D. Merilee Clunis, PhD
Karen I. Fredriksen-Gol
Pat A. Freeman, PhD
Nancy M. Nystrom, PhD

Lives of Lesbian Elders
Looking Back,
Looking Forward

Pre-publication
REVIEWS,
COMMENTARIES,
EVALUATIONS . . .

More pre-publication
REVIEWS, COMMENTARIES, EVALUATIONS . . .

"*L*ives of Lesbian Elders, written by academics from the fields of social work, history, and psychology, provides an inspirational account of older lesbians, ranging in age from fifty-five to ninety-five, living in the states of Washington, Oregon, and California. Despite facing the challenges of the triad of ageism, sexism, and homophobia, these women typify fortitude and their stories will leave readers shocked, saddened, stirred, and hopeful.

Written from a strengths perspective, *Lives of Lesbian Elders* offers younger lesbian readers heartfelt guidance from older lesbians. This book does an exceptional job of demonstrating how historical and social contexts of different time periods influence sexual orientation identity development.

This book will appeal to a wide audience, including people who care about the elderly and those who are interested in the lives of lesbians during a time in our history when prescriptive gender role expectations limited the work and romantic lives of women."

Elizabeth P. Cramer, PhD, LCSW, ACSW
Associate Professor, Virginia
Commonwealth University
School of Social Work;
Editor, *Addressing Homophobia
and Heterosexism
on College Campuses*

The Haworth Press®
New York • London • Oxford

Lives of Lesbian Elders
Looking Back,
Looking Forward

HAWORTH Innovations in Feminist Studies
J. Dianne Garner
Senior Editor

Lives of Lesbian Elders
Looking Back,
Looking Forward

D. Merilee Clunis, PhD
Karen I. Fredriksen-Goldsen, PhD
Pat A. Freeman, PhD
Nancy M. Nystrom, PhD

The Haworth Press®
New York • London • Oxford

The Haworth Press, Inc., 10 Alice Street, Binghamton, NY 13904-1580.

PUBLISHER'S NOTE
Identities and circumstances of individuals discussed in this book have been changed to protect confidentiality.

Cover design by Kerry E. Mack.

Library of Congress Cataloging-in-Publication Data

Lives of lesbian elders : looking back, looking forward / D. Merilee Clunis [et al.].
    p. cm.
    Based on interviews with 62 lesbians ranging in age from 55 to 95 and residing in California, Oregon, and Washington State.
    Includes bibliographical references and index.
    ISBN 0-7890-2333-4 (hard : alk. paper)—ISBN 0-7890-2334-2 (soft : alk. paper).
    1. Middle aged lesbians—United States—Attitudes. 2. Aged lesbians—United States—Attitudes. 3. Lesbianism—United States—Public opinion. 4. Public opinion—United States. 5. Lesbians—United States—Social conditions. I. Title: Lesbian elders : looking back, looking forward. II. Clunis, D. Merilee.
HQ75.6.U5L58 2004
306.76'63'0922—dc22
                                                              2003028212

To all those who came before us

ABOUT THE AUTHORS

D. Merilee Clunis, PhD, is co-author of *Lesbian Couples: A Guide to Creating Healthy Relationships* and *The Lesbian Parenting Book: A Guide to Creating Families and Raising Children.* She has published and conducted workshops on communication, training, couple relationships, and parenting. Dr. Clunis is in private practice in Seattle, Washington.

Karen I. Fredriksen-Goldsen, PhD, is co-author of *Families and Work: New Directions in the Twenty-First Century.* She is Director of the Institute for Multigenerational Health, Development, and Equality and is Associate Professor of Social Work at the University of Washington in Seattle. Dr. Fredriksen-Goldsen is a past recipient of the Outstanding Research Award by the Society for Social Work and Research and has been published extensively on intergenerational caregiving, work and family, and family care within nontraditional families.

Pat A. Freeman, PhD, is actively involved with the Northwest LGBT History Project. He has done numerous presentations on gay/lesbian history for high schools, universities, and community organizations. Since his female-to-male (FTM) transition, Dr. Freeman has shifted his focus to include transgender issues.

Nancy Nystrom, PhD, is Assistant Professor in the School of Social Work at Michigan State University in East Lansing, where she teaches aging policy, community organizing, social work policy, and social work practice. She is an intern for Old Lesbians Organizing for Change, and is a member of the National Gay and Lesbian Task Force Policy Institute, the American Society on Aging, and the National Organization of Gay and Lesbian Scientists.

CONTENTS

Preface and Acknowledgments

This book emerged from conversations with lesbian elders. Although we were from different academic backgrounds, namely history, psychology, and social work, the six of us shared the view that these women's stories and history were—and are—being lost, and that loss means our link to our understanding of our past and future is jeopardized. We decided to embark on a project we called "Looking Back, Looking Forward," which we hoped would help bring our lesbian elders out of the shadows, restore our history, and provide at least some of the information necessary to meet the future needs of aging lesbians.

In those early meetings we shared our visions, clarified our goals, honed our focus, and made decisions. We determined the goal of the project would be to provide accounts of the experiences of lesbian elders against the backdrop of the historical context of their times. Thus, what they did and why they did it (for example, avoiding the term "lesbian") becomes clearer with an understanding of how homosexuality was perceived and treated during the early 1900s through the 1960s.

All six of us were involved in setting the initial purpose and scope of the project. We decided to limit our sample to women age fifty-five and older, to include those living in Washington, Oregon, and California, and to gather information through in-person interviews. We developed a semistructured interview based on a set of open-ended questions that could be completed in one to one and a half hours. Participants were gathered primarily through snowball sampling, and the taped interviews were conducted in their homes during 1997 and 1998. To analyze the material, we first transcribed the interviews and then at least two of us coded each one to identify themes.

All of the initial members of the team remained with the project into the data-gathering phase until one member, Pat Terry, needed to leave due to other commitments. Another member, Teresa Jones, stayed with the project through the data-analysis phase when, as anticipated, her professional obligations necessitated her pulling back.

The four remaining members of the project—Merilee Clunis, Karen Fredriksen-Goldsen, Pat Freeman, and Nancy Nystrom—are responsible for creating this book from the interviews. We have tried to understand what these lesbian elders were saying about themselves, their lives, and their social and historical context. And we have tried to convey that understanding, as much as possible, in their own words. We feel privileged that these women were willing to share their stories with us. We sincerely hope that we have reflected them accurately and that their response to the book will be, "Yes. They heard us."

We have many people to thank for their help in creating this book. First and foremost, we want to thank the lesbian elders whose words and lives appear in this book. We have profound respect for their trials and tribulations and the deepest gratitude for their willingness to open their lives to us.

We are also indebted to the Pride Foundation of Seattle for the grant that allowed us to have the interviews transcribed; to Jennie Goode, who provided invaluable editing and advice on earlier versions of most of the chapters; to our families for their support throughout this project; and to one another for persevering during the time it took to complete this book.

Introduction

My strength comes from my desire. . . . I have a desire to grow in grace.

Ernestine, age seventy-five

GETTING STARTED

The lives of elder lesbians have simply been overlooked. As women, as lesbians, and as elders they have been stigmatized and marginalized by U.S. society. Their lives have largely remained invisible in a society that, through much of the twentieth century, criminalized homosexuality in order to enforce heterosexuality. Despite this, the sixty-two lesbians, ranging in age from fifty-five to ninety-five, interviewed for this book have lived dynamic lives, drawing upon their resourcefulness, amazing resilience, and independence. Unfortunately, their stories are being lost to time; without them our link to the past as well as our understanding of the future is in jeopardy. With professional backgrounds in psychology, social work, and history, the authors began the "Looking Back, Looking Forward" project as a means to bring our lesbian elders out of the shadows and restore their history, one piece of the collective history of lesbians in the United States.

In the early stages of this project, we developed a semistructured interview based on a set of open-ended questions, designed to take approximately an hour to an hour and a half. We searched for older lesbians to interview, but it was difficult finding willing participants. Notices in gay/lesbian publications produced few responses. We have little doubt that older lesbians' reluctance to be interviewed reflected the impact of the stigma of being gay during the era in which these women were coming of age. The fear and distrust that was so much a part of being lesbian remained strong, especially for those over sixty-

1

five years of age. As a result, confidentiality was of particular concern. From the few older lesbians willing to be interviewed, we gathered other names. We contacted these women to explain the project and solicit referrals to others who might be interested in participating.

Many women granted interviews only after we had established credibility, trust, and fellowship through the process of direct contact. However, as we built trust with each referral and interview, more referrals followed. Although this approach to obtaining participants was successful, it also had drawbacks. The major risk was that this "snowball sampling" might skew the demographics because of the tendency for people to associate with those of similar age, socioeconomic class, and ethnicity. Despite this potential drawback, the sample was, in fact, quite diverse in income, education, and age. Many of these referrals also added to the geographic diversity of the group, providing contacts throughout California, Oregon, and Washington.

Personal referrals did open doors, but they did not open all doors. The project team was diverse in terms of class background and race, yet only about 5 percent of those interviewed were lesbians of color. Life expectancies are generally lower for populations of color, so there may be proportionately fewer of these elders. More important reasons, however, included fear of discovery as well as outright distrust of researchers. One woman of color stated that she had been interviewed for one of the very first lesbian studies, had been misquoted, and felt used. She did not trust researchers—lesbian or otherwise.

Aside from being lesbian, the women who participated in this study differed in other ways from the stereotypical woman of the time. For example, women generally were not encouraged to attend college; they were, however, expected to get married. Even after World War II's GI Bill opened college campuses in greater numbers to women, society decreed that women should attend for no longer than two years—the time expected to find a suitable husband. Although the women interviewed were diverse in terms of class background and income, a surprising number had attended college. Twenty-nine percent of the women interviewed had some college; 21 percent had an undergraduate college degree; 43 percent had a graduate degree; and 7 percent had a high school diploma or less.

More than 50 percent of the women had been married and 42 percent had children. Of these, some had acknowledged their lesbianism but had given in to social pressures and married. Others had repressed their lesbianism, especially to themselves, and had married. A few had admitted their lesbianism, at least to themselves, but stayed married until after their children were grown, and then divorced.

Fifty-three percent of the women were retired from a job or career. However, they continued to do volunteer work, hold full- and/or part-time positions, and pursue education, hobbies, travel, and a variety of interests. For these women, retirement has not led to stasis. Their household incomes ranged from $10,000 to over $100,000. Of the 47 percent who had not yet retired, a number continued to work well into their sixties. One woman had no immediate intention to retire even though she was in her early eighties. Ninety-four percent of the women described their health as good or excellent, although 17 percent acknowledged serious health problems or a major disability. Sixty-five percent of the women had partners; 35 percent were single or their partners had died. Geographically, 37 percent lived in California, 36 percent in Washington, and 27 percent in Oregon.

In putting this book together, we recognized that what the women had to say was the most important aspect of it. To that end we have quoted them extensively; however, we have not quoted equally from all sixty-two interviews. Rather, we selected quotes that were representative of a particular experience. As promised, we have changed the women's names and identifying information for reasons of confidentiality. Generally the women told us that being interviewed was a rewarding experience, even a freeing one. We, too, benefited tremendously from this process. Meeting these women, all of whom were, intentionally or not, pioneers in the gay movement, was exciting and memorable. We thank them for the privilege of being allowed to share their lives, for even a short time.

The life experiences of these lesbian elders provide the basic material for this book. How these women lived—the choices they made and their reasons for making them—can be understood only within the context of the changing perception of homosexuality throughout the twentieth century. Thus, historical background is central to this project.

HISTORICAL BACKGROUND

Early History

If we are to understand the importance of these elder voices and the significance of their message in today's world, we must listen to them within the context of their time, not from the perspective of the twenty-first century. We must understand the culture, the politics, and the social mores of the eras in which these women came of age. Each of us is the product of history, and the women here are no different.

If coming of age is defined as the years leading up to and including the generally defined legal age of twenty-one—the years that shape and establish a person's identity—then familiarity with the history of the years spanning 1900 through 1969 is necessary in order to comprehend the lives of the women in this book. If we are to understand the fear, rebellion, compromise, loss, resiliency, courage, and tenacity it required to be lesbian prior to the late 1980s, we must not lose sight of the fact that to be homosexual was to be considered a pariah, a criminal, and/or a sick individual subject to voluntary or involuntary medical cures, including lobotomy. Above all, if we are to understand the events and forces that shaped these women, we must approach their chronicle from the social history of lesbians in the twentieth century.

Up until the early 1900s, lesbianism was viewed as a relatively innocuous occurrence that prepared women for "real sex," that is, sex with a man. A woman who maintained a long-term relationship with another woman was said to be in a Boston marriage. This term conferred respectability to the relationship between two women—generally educated and of the financially secure middle or upper classes—who lived together in what was considered a marriage and thus helped to keep them from becoming a social and/or economic burden to their families.

Often one woman assumed a more assertive, masculine role and dressed in a masculine fashion while the other assumed a more feminine role, dressed accordingly, and ran the household. The Ladies of Llangollen—Eleanor Butler and Sarah Ponsonby (who had a more-than-fifty-year relationship)—are an example of such an arrangement, as are Willa Cather and Edith Lewis (together for forty years). Novelist Sarah Orne Jewett and Annie Fields; Irish writer Edith

Somerville and Violet Martin; Rosa Bonheur (painter) and Nathalie Micas; and Mary Woolley (president of Mount Holyoke College) and Jeanette Marks provide additional illustrations of these committed relationships.

Women during this period had few rights outside the control of a male family member or husband. However, those in Boston marriages achieved more independence and control over their lives. In addition, a growing number of young upper- and middle-class women were attending women's colleges, and articles in popular magazines and newspapers endorsed and promoted the many benefits of education and special friendships.

The early 1900s saw an increasing prosperity in the United States, which led to a growing middle class with a strong sense of social and political responsibility and a mounting sense of optimism. In spite of their prominent involvement in such progressive movement reforms as child labor, banking regulation, and food standards, people in the middle classes found time to indulge in their increasing interest in the medically "deviant" and "grotesque." For instance, Magnus Hirschfeld, Sigmund Freud, and Havelock Ellis were publishing studies about flagellation, sadomasochism, homosexuality, and the like.

After 1910, as a result of the medicalization of lesbianism and the growing public knowledge of the "dangers" of lesbianism to young women, the popular media no longer looked favorably on women's education and independence. College-bound young women and their parents were now warned of the temptations and corruption awaiting them: depravities that von Krafft-Ebing, Ellis, and Freud had added to the psychological/medical lexicon and the vocabulary of the knowledgeable public, along with the terms "homosexual" and "lesbian."

The public heeded the warnings. Increased newspaper coverage and very visible police raids of bars, balls, and clubs catering to gays and lesbians became almost indispensable in keeping the majority heterosexual society aware of the homosexual threat to the country's morals. Such stories and incidents likely increased the sale of newspapers—and in the process reinforced the message that deviance would not be allowed. Now that homosexuality was linked to mental illness and the criminal world, visibility, however limited, was no longer tolerated.

In the glare of such public knowledge and scrutiny of the perverse, any single, independent, professional woman was often assumed to be a lesbian. For lesbians seeking protection in Queen Victoria's apocryphal dictate that lesbians did not exist, invisibility neither ensured safety nor provided peace of mind. In fact, public suspicions about the relationships of women educators, such as Mary Woolley and Jeannette Marks of Mount Holyoke College, and M. Carey Thomas and Mary Garrett of Bryn Mawr College, led to their discomfort, fear, and change of living arrangements.

Young men, also, did not escape examination. They were admonished to be manly and to avoid the "sink" of pansyism that had been personified earlier by Oscar Wilde and had so shocked society on both continents. No longer was it acceptable for men to engage in sex with an effeminate male, or "pansy," as a substitute for sex with a woman. What before had been passed off simply as a means to satisfy the natural drives of men when women were not available was now viewed as evidence of perversion.

World War I

The forming and reforming of political and military alliances such as the Franco-Russian Alliance and the Triple Entente, as well as the escalating crisis in Morocco in 1911, set in motion ominous rumbles in Europe. When war broke out, the developing war technology quickly killed the men and the horses they rode. It killed the French soldiers in their bright blue tunics, who marched into battle in disciplined formation. It killed Englishmen, Germans, and, when the United States entered the war in 1918, it killed the doughboys. The war changed the world. Europe was devastated and struggled to rebuild. Germany was burdened by enormous debt. The United States became a creditor nation with loans and investments in Europe.

America was changed. Like it or not, the country was now part of the international scene—no more isolation. The growing public sophistication that came from greater involvement in other parts of the world led to an increasing awareness of same-sex love. The troops had spent time in Paris. Gays and lesbians met others like themselves; they frequented homosexual clubs, and many experienced Parisian society, which was more tolerant and accepting of homosexuality. After the war the question for Americans (gay, lesbian, and straight) was now, "How do you keep 'em down on the farm after they've seen Paree?"

The answer was: You did not. Straights and gays returning from the war migrated to the larger cities in search of opportunities or simply as an antidote to the sameness and predictability of farm and small-town life. Gays and lesbians, in particular, sought the more tolerant climate of the larger cities where they were more likely to meet others like themselves. Automobiles and trains provided mobility for all classes of society and changed the way people lived and played.

New York, Chicago, and San Francisco, all with reputations of "anything goes," became meccas for the avant-garde, bohemians, and gays and lesbians, as did Greenwich Village and Harlem in New York, South Side Chicago, and the Tenderloin in San Francisco. Jazz, blues, bathtub gin, speakeasies, drag balls, sin, sex, masculine women, and effeminate men proliferated. Bessie Smith and Ma Rainey defied convention and shouted out that they may "say I do it, ain't nobody caught me, sure got to prove it on me . . ." And Gladys Bentley—all 300 pounds of her, in white tuxedo and top hat—attracted long lines of whites, blacks, straights, and gays to her shows. Nobody played the piano and sang like Gladys. She was the queen of the dirty ditty, double entendre, and low-down blues.

Reform in the Air

Although it is the bobbed-hair and bathtub gin set that seems to have left its mark on the postwar years, these people were not, in fact, representative of the majority of society. The older middle-class majority found such fast-living antics deplorable at best. Certainly the hobnobbing and sexual experimenting going on in the big cities was evidence to the majority that society was in decline. Legal means and social pressures were used to counteract what many feared to be an increase in homosexuality. Such lowering of morals was directly due, many believed, to homosexuals being allowed to serve in the military and to the corrupting influences of foreign lands.

The morally righteous found confirmation of America's decline in the events of the Newport Naval Station scandal of 1919. The business community and moral reformers, concerned about the large number of effeminate sailors who cruised the Cliff Walk and congregated at the local YMCA brazenly soliciting homosexual sex, supported the U.S. Navy in a homosexual witch-hunt. The navy sent out "decoys," entrapped the sailors, and charged them with criminal acts of sodomy, drug use, and the like. In keeping with the mores of the times, the "decoys," who openly testified to having had sexual relations (which some said they enjoyed) with the sailors in question, experienced no repercussions, no stigma, no questions of ethics. Not one of these more masculine men who the sailors serviced faced arrest or prosecution. This fact speaks volumes about the period regarding homosexuality and the attribution of specific sexual acts to gender roles; that is, the "manly" man was considered manly as long as he was serviced by an effeminate man; it was the effeminate man who went against nature. The message of the entrapment and prosecution of the sailors by the Department of the Navy was not lost to lesbians: It was another reason to move further into invisibility even though women were rarely if ever arrested and prosecuted.

The reformers also targeted the tolerant atmosphere of the big cities, which they believed encouraged sin. It was in this atmosphere that Henry Gerber and six of his friends founded the Society for Human Rights in Chicago in 1924 (the earliest documented homosexual emancipation organization in the United States) with the goals of educating the public and bringing about legal reform. They also published a journal, *Friendship and Freedom,* which reported on the society's activities. In 1925 police raided Gerber's house and confiscated his papers. He and other members of the society were arrested and jailed for three days without charges. Gerber lost his job and the society was disbanded.

Not surprisingly, during this period so-called patriotic societies flourished. These right-wing conservative groups used intimidation to promote white power through the control of education, business, and the public at large. The Ku Klux Klan experienced rapid growth and held picnics and massive hooded parades. Less civilized activities included cross burnings, beatings, and lynchings. They focused their hate on blacks, Catholics, Jews, immigrants, and homosexuals.

While the market, despite some warning signs, continued to gain, the moral reformers did not. The high living, speakeasy hopping, drag ball attending, drug and sex experimenting of the young and the Gatsby set appeared to be on the rise. Even *The Well of Loneliness,* banned in England and declared by the conservative *Sunday Express* to be nothing but an "unutterable putrefaction" (Omrod, 1985, p. 177) was published in the United States—and worse yet was being widely read. The reformers need not have worried, however. Its author,

Radclyffe Hall, believed in the theories of Ellis (namely that "inverts" were born that way and destined to be miserable) and von Krafft-Ebing (1969, pp. 222-225) (who believed inversion resulted in "anti-pathic sexual instinct," even though he did support efforts to repeal Paragraph 175 of the German law that made sexual relations between adult males a crime). In melodramatic style, Hall espoused Ellis's theories in particular. Her novel's turgid prose and depressing plot portrays a lonely, mannish lesbian doomed to a life of seeking "the love that dare not speak its name" (Wilde, 1960, p. 41). Shunned and enduring social condemnation, she learns that nature, i.e., heterosexuality, will triumph.

The extent of *The Well of Loneliness*'s influence on lesbians of the 1920s through the 1960s is difficult to assess. Although the book presented a negative portrayal of lesbian life, it was still a representation of lesbians. Even if many lesbians found the novel to be depressing at best, its depiction of Parisian lesbian enclaves showed that all lesbians were not living lives of anguish. Just how many lesbians who read Hall's book recognized that Valerie Seymour was based on the American expatriate Natalie Barney, or that the descriptions of the gay bars were exceedingly accurate, is obviously unknown—and in the long run does not matter. What is important is that, for better or worse, *The Well of Loneliness* showed that resistance to heterosexual conformity was a real possibility. This resistance was manifested in a number of ways, especially in finding and meeting others, in spite of the very real dangers of discovery.

Another significant message conveyed by the book was this: The U.S. public received confirmation that lesbians were predatory and perverse and, worse yet, mannish. With much hue and cry, the defenders of public morals announced that the publication of Hall's novel was but further proof that the decline and fall of the United States was but one perverse act away. Government passed and enforced laws that criminalized homosexuals and drove them underground. Even worse, some lesbians accepted lesbian life as described by Hall; they embraced it, took it as their truth, and were frightened by what it portrayed.

Crash and Reform: The End of Gatsby

By 1919 Berlin had replaced Paris as the "open city" of Europe. The city's temptations and vices appeared in guidebooks such as *What's Not in the Baedeker Guide, 1927*. Magnus Hirschfeld's Institute of Sexology provided scientific public lectures, research, medical care for sexual dysfunction, and a very popular museum of sexual aides, which was a major attraction for tourists—homosexual and heterosexual. Homosexuality flourished in this atmosphere. But in 1933, in an economy wracked by a worldwide depression, unemployment at devastatingly high levels, and merciless inflation, Hitler came to power.

FDR won the 1932 presidential election and Hitler seized power in January 1933. The Great Depression was, of course, a world depression that saw the rise of fascism in the United States as well as in Europe. Black Shirts marched in Italy, Brown Shirts marched in Germany, and Silver Shirts marched in the United States. In Germany, Hitler denounced Jews, homosexuals, and international bankers. In 1935, under the guise of reining in unfettered hedonism and restoring family values, Hitler acted on the authority of the newly amended paragraph 175 of the criminal code and began the Nazi roundup and imprisonment of homosexuals.

In the United States, Father Charles Coughlin denounced Jews and international bankers, and—along with other moral reformers—condemned homosexuals. Banks failed, unemployment grew exponentially as did lines at soup kitchens, and men abandoned families to hop the rails or build Hoovervilles. Fascism in the form of Father Coughlin and his radio broadcasts gained huge audiences. The American fascist Silver Shirt movement increased its membership nationwide. Moral reformers and politicians, cognizant of the power to be gained by warning of the ever-present dangers of nonconforming groups including homosexuals, busily investigated these groups looking to reform anything they designated as morally lax or corrupt. Vilification by the press and public guaranteed that homosexuals (male and female) were viewed as criminals unable to escape their own perversities. In the meantime, the masses sought relief from business failures, unemployment, bank failures, family breakups, and overwhelming poverty.

In Europe, World War II broke out in 1939 with the Nazi invasion of Poland. History tends to repeat itself in many ways. The war years were no exception, and many social and economic changes occurred as a result of World War II. During the war, women joined the factory workforce in great numbers. Rosie the Riveter became the symbol of the new woman. She was independent and could do a man's job. The military, too, offered women the opportunity to join, which they did—including lesbians in large numbers. But just as after World War I, when the war ended, women were turned out of their jobs and told to become housewives. The government actively promoted policies and advertising campaigns encouraging women to return to the home.

After the War: Conformity

The congressional elections of 1946 brought in a Republican-controlled Congress that sought to control the unions and prevent an apparent spread of communism. Such distrust of Russia's intentions and politics following the Russian expansion into Berlin led to ever-growing suspicions and fears in the United States. Reacting, in part, to fear of impending destruction and the potential impotency of American might, society displayed less and less tolerance for those seen as different, and homosexuals were at the top of the list. In magazines geared to the general public, the psychiatric and mental health communities published articles extolling the benefits of normalcy and the destructiveness of being abnormal, that is, homosexual—a condition that could be cured, of course, by the compassionate psychiatrist or mental health worker.

Unfortunately, some of the cures offered, for example, shock treatment and lobotomy, often had destructive side effects; others were simply time-consuming, ineffectual, and very expensive. Some homosexuals were involuntarily treated, sanctioned by criminal and mental health laws. With homosexuals treated as criminals and social deviants, at risk of losing their jobs, credit, social standing, friends, and subject to blackmail and involuntary commitment, it is not surprising that gays and lesbians moved ever further into what is now referred to as the "closet." They formed a rapidly growing and vast underground subculture and stayed there out of fear.

Although the majority of the medical community supported the current beliefs of the times, some sought change. The 1948 and 1953 publications of Alfred Kinsey's studies of sexual behavior in men and women, which reported that 8 percent of men were homosexual and 28 percent of women had erotic responses to women, shocked America. Unfortunately, they failed to enlighten the public, most of whom had not actually read the books. The studies had a limited impact within the medical profession as well. The fear of difference, whether in sexuality or politics, ran rampant in American society.

As fear of communism—which, with the help of the media and right-wing politicians was becoming linked in the public mind with homosexuality, blackmail, un-Americanism, and perversity—increased, so did loyalty oath requirements for government and public educational institutions. Many states formed committees to investigate the nefarious activities of myriad communists, and by association homosexuals, in such places as government, Hollywood, universities, and the military. In the early 1950s, Joseph McCarthy, a Republican senator from Wisconsin, was appointed chairman of an investigative arm of the Senate Committee on Government Operations. With Roy Cohn as chief counsel, McCarthy charged that the State Department was riddled with communists and perverts (homosexuals), and that there was, in fact, a list of 205 names. McCarthy then proceeded to intimidate politicians, the military, and the public at large.

Few stood up to McCarthy. Most joined in the paranoia and, if called to testify before his committee, named names. Considered to be security risks, gays and lesbians were fired from government service jobs; gay and lesbian teachers were fired as corrupters of children; gays and lesbians were also fired from civilian jobs and evicted from apartments. The military stepped up its search for homosexuals in the ranks and dishonorably discharged them. McCarthy reportedly died of cirrhosis of the liver, likely a result of alcoholism, in 1957. Unfortunately, however, homophobia did not die with McCarthy. Cohn was disbarred shortly before his death in 1986 of AIDS-related cancer. He'd lived a deeply closeted life, denying his homosexuality in spite of being notorious for picking up hustlers.

There was opposition to the homophobic hysteria. Psychologist Evelyn Hooker conducted a series of studies of gay men in 1956 that challenged the accepted dogma of homosexuality as a mental disorder. In 1957 in England, the Wolfenden Report stated, "homosexual behavior between consenting adults in private should no longer be a criminal offense" (Miller, 1995, p. 283). Homophile organizations such as the Daughters of Bilitis and the Mattachine Society, which published the magazine *ONE,* did exist. However, most gays and lesbians were not tempted to move out of the closet by such reports or organizations.

As is true about so much of life, economic and social status had much to do with how one lived—in this case, in or out of the closet. The famous and the rich led amazingly open lives as, indeed, they had always done. For example, Dorothy Arzner, a film director from the 1920s to the 1940s, was recognized as a lesbian by the movie industry. Marlene Dietrich's affairs and her relationship with Mercedes de Acosta were well inferred among those "in the know." The movie-viewing public was meanwhile subjected to massive publicity campaigns showing Dietrich smiling happily in heterosexual romantic situations. The wealthy and upper middle class also managed, for the most part, to maintain their way of life. They held private parties and went to San Francisco, the Village, and Cherry Grove, the oldest town on Fire Island. If life began to be marked by galloping ennui, they simply went to Europe.

Working-class gays and lesbians did not have such options and led more restricted lives, many finding their social life in "the bars." The Volstead Act (prohibition), originally passed in 1919 and generally ignored until the 1930s, actually opened the door nationwide for a more entrenched police payoff system that allowed speakeasies to flourish and furthered East Coast expansion by the Mafia who began running bars catering to homosexuals. A similar non-Mafia payoff system on the West Coast also allowed such bars to operate. Women who frequented the bars were subjected to the "butch/femme" dogmatism that dominated bar culture. For many women, however, bars and the gay scene were not an option for either meeting other lesbians or simply socializing in a gay/lesbian atmosphere. The women in this study often discovered lesbianism (their own or someone else's) at college or on the job.

Whether they were working, middle, or upper class, lesbians and gays often lived with guilt, denial, and fear. The parties and bars provided a semblance of safety and a place to mingle. There was, indeed, an atmosphere of camaraderie, acceptance, and solidarity, but it came at a price. Alcohol flowed freely. Its consumption allowed one to for-

get the everyday pain of living a lie, of constantly hiding the truth
from society and from oneself. It filled the glasses of the lonely solitary drinkers as well. In the end, class did not protect gays and lesbians from alcoholism or loneliness, which flourished in their communities. And the closet door remained as tightly shut as ever.

Denial, social pressure, and fear of discovery led many gays and
lesbians to voluntarily seek instantaneous heterosexuality at the hands
of therapists and psychiatrists who practiced a variety of techniques
to cure homosexuality. Others were forced into medical treatment by
spouses, parents, friends, "concerned" citizens (e.g., doctors or educators), or the criminal justice system. Others found avoidance of the
mental health professionals to be safer, easier, cheaper, and less traumatic: They just got married. As previously noted, more than half of
the lesbians in this study married. The reasons included not recognizing their lesbianism, doing what was expected, suppressing lesbian
desires, and marrying because of pregnancy or the desire to have children.

The Movements

After the Kennedy assassination, when the women's movement,
the Vietnam War, the Stonewall riots, and the start of the gay liberation movement turned American society upside down, younger gays
and lesbians began to emerge from the closet. However, for the majority of older gays and lesbians these changes were not enough and
they remained silenced.

Younger gays and lesbians, in particular, had learned from the civil
rights movement and were no longer willing to accept denigration or
invisibility. In Seattle, Washington, in 1967, several owners of gay
bars rebelled against the police payoff system and testified against
the police department. The chief of police was forced to resign and
several policemen received jail sentences. This activism ended the
payoff system as well as the policy of harassment of gay bars in Seattle.

Two years later at the Stonewall Inn—a seedy bar in Greenwich
Village, New York, noted primarily for its "nothing left to lose" pa-
trons including hustlers, queens, and the down-and-out—a few queens
and dykes stood up to the police and refused to load themselves pas-
sively into the waiting paddy wagons. They threw pennies, chanted,

sang, and set the bar on fire. The Stonewall riots, which lasted five days in varying incarnations, marked the start of what has come to be known as the gay liberation movement.

The removal of homosexuality from the *Diagnostic and Statistical Manual of Mental Disorders* in 1973 reflected a shift in social opinion and simultaneously contributed to further change. In this more supportive atmosphere mental health service providers did not necessarily become gay and lesbian affirmative, but many formerly closeted therapists and members of the medical professions began coming out professionally.

Gay and lesbian activists began sponsoring gay/lesbian dances and events, and university students joined in support. Laws allowing involuntary commitment were changed. "Out" gays and lesbians entered politics in surprisingly large numbers and were elected, also in surprisingly large numbers. Today gay and lesbian liberation is still evolving. Visibility continues to grow as more are stepping forward and coming out. More gays and lesbians have moved into the mainstream, some with children and homes in the suburbs. Even though a lesbian, gay, bisexual, and transgender presence is gaining public support, a very real and growing form of virulent homophobia and heterosexism remains and must not be ignored. As history reveals, complacency can be dangerous.

In this book the importance of the historical context of the women's lives cannot be overstated. Understanding the periods during which the women came of age and first recognized their lesbianism is essential because their history continues to shape their lives today. As highlighted throughout this introduction, the women came of age at a time when homosexuality was severely stigmatized and lesbian invisibility reigned. Few public portrayals of lesbian life were in existence, and those few depicted a life of despair, shame, and loneliness. Understanding history is the key to where we've been, knowing who we are and what challenges the future may bring. Only through listening to the voices of the lesbian elders themselves can we learn about their experiences—and our collective history—and come to appreciate their strengths and needs as they age.

These women are the forerunners to the gay liberation movement. Without their sacrifices and resolve, we would not be where we are today. Through looking back and looking forward, the women shared their lives—the dreams, the compromises, and the simple truths.

Chapter 1

Coming Out

The parades and the fact that there were organizations and people were talking about it finally . . . suddenly I felt free.

Madelyn, age ninety-five

During the period that most of the women in this book came of age—from the 1920s to the 1960s—lesbian invisibility was the norm. At the time many of the women in this study were discovering their lesbianism, the term "invert" and the image of the masculine, predatory lesbian destined to live a life of misery were well established in the public mind. Despite the severe social stigma attached to homosexuality, a number of books about lesbians, such as Colette's *Cheri* series, were translated into English in the 1930s and became available, although not easily accessible.

Women of the time reacted to these materials in a variety of ways: they accessed, ignored, or treasured these portrayals of lesbian life. Because of the conservatism of the era, those coming of age in the 1950s had even less information available to them than had their predecessors. As evident in the introduction to this book, there were more reasons to stay "in the closet" than to be out during these times. The process of "coming out" is complex at any time, but for women during the first half of the twentieth century, coming out to oneself or to a few select friends was a very difficult process, though not without its own rewards.

This chapter explores how older lesbians define coming out and what influenced their decisions regarding whether, and to what extent, to publicly acknowledge their lesbianism. In reality, many of the women we interviewed had little choice about whether to come out. Most had two options: repression or secrecy. Thus, many denied their lesbianism to themselves and sought to repress their attraction to women, often through marriage and motherhood. Others maintained a facade of heterosexuality and secretly lived an underground lesbian life. A very few lived a relatively open lesbian life despite the social pressures of the times. As the liberation movements of the late 1960s and the 1970s increased levels of tolerance and acceptance, some of the women increased their visibility in later life; for others, it was not an option.

COMING OUT: WHAT DOES IT MEAN?

When asked what coming out meant to them, none of the women professed ignorance of the term, but they did define it in many ways. For a great many the phrase indicated being public about their lesbianism, which the majority had not done and did not plan to do. Many described the idea of coming out publicly with apprehension or even disapproval. They described it as "exposing my lifestyle to the rest of the world" or "flaunting my private business for all the world to see." Some of those who equated coming out with making a public declaration did not think of themselves as ever having come out—even if they had gay friends or had eventually disclosed their lesbianism to family members or straight friends.

Charlotte, now sixty-seven, described herself as having been in the closet for "some sixty years."

> I don't feel I ever came out because I come from an era, as you know . . . it was a closeted era. Since I've retired, my attitude has changed and I think I'm coming—I mean, hell, everybody knew I was gay. Who cared? I've lived with my present friend for thirty-two years. Have a wild and woolly history in my past, and worked at the same place for forty years. So I don't know if I can explain any more than probably [coming out] is just letting your hair down. But I'm not the type of person who's going to run out on the corner and say, "Hey, look, I'm gay."

Given the times in which many of these women acknowledged or acted on their same-sex attractions, even discussing it with anyone was often out of the question. The risk of humiliation, rejection, and ostracism was too great. Besides, they did not discuss such personal matters: It was no one else's business.

Rita, age seventy-seven, grew up on a farm and then moved to New York City, where she enjoyed the excitement of the urban atmosphere. She was aware that some of the artists with whom she regularly associated were gay, but that fact was never discussed. Eventually she moved to the West Coast, where she now lives with her friend of forty years. She describes herself as clear about who she is and comfortable with her lesbian identity, but not out.

> "Coming out" to me means public acknowledgment—which I've never done. . . . I didn't have any particular need to discuss it. . . . I have, wherever I've lived, I've assumed—I think quite rightly—that many people [were] aware, but I was not specifically demonstrating my position. I think at the time, and I still feel, it is nobody else's business, and yet I feel that those who have come out are freer people. . . . Whether it was my determination to ignore or my fear, I don't know, but I wasn't terribly alert or aware of [gay/lesbian life]. Probably [involved] some denial or avoidance.

Although many believed that their biological family members were aware of their lesbianism, most of the women had not formally come out to their parents. Siblings, especially sisters, were often most approachable. Those who had married and had children often kept their lesbianism a secret, telling their children only after they were grown.

Almost without exception these older lesbians remained closeted on the job. Whether their work was professional, white collar, or blue collar, they believed they could not be out. For many, being more public about their sexual orientation became a possibility only after they retired.

Rhonda, age sixty, now retired from a career in the military, defined coming out as involving her relationship both with herself and with the world.

> Well, it means being myself, being comfortable with myself enough so that I will come out, as appropriate. . . . It means being clear that I know who I am and I'm okay to be who I am with the world. . . . It's been hard. Having served in the military—I've been with a woman since I was twenty-two—so certainly I was uncomfortable coming out to anybody but my partner. So that

was a long process of [becoming] comfortable with talking to
friends even. And the coming out to parents didn't happen until
I was forty-one. And now—it's been a long process, but now
I'm comfortable coming out to most everybody. I don't just
stand up and say, "I'm a lesbian." But I come out as [is] socially
appropriate.

Rather than emphasizing the public aspect, some women defined
coming out as a more personal, individual process through which
they became aware of who they were, acknowledged their sexual orientation to themselves, and became comfortable with it. For example,
Mary Alice, age sixty-eight, experienced a year-and-a-half-long relationship with a woman when she was fourteen. The relationship was
so intense that they didn't dare touch each other because they felt that
if they did, they would die or "something transformational would occur." And then when she was seventeen, she had her first physical en-
counter with a woman. She used an analogy to describe what coming
out meant to her.

It was like coming from the stage of the cocoon to a butterfly.
It's a process. It's like from one way of being to another way of
being. And more than that, though, it was to know who I was—
really know who I was for the first time. Just—ah! It was like an
"aha."

For some, like Mary Alice, this transformation happened fairly
quickly. For most of the women, however, the process occurred over
many years.

THE CLOSET

Fear of being discovered made coming out a prolonged and frequently circuitous process for many older lesbians. Some remained
closeted, others ventured out later in life, and still others came out
and then returned to the closet. "Blending," or being totally closeted,
was as often the result of an acceptance of lesbianism as perverse as it
was an avoidance of society's punitive mores. The denial involved in
never discussing lesbianism includes saying to oneself and everyone

else, "I am not that!" Such disavowal leads to a life overshadowed by repression and fear.

At ninety-five years of age, Madelyn was the oldest woman interviewed and the one with the longest experience of a closeted life. At the time of the interview she lived in a nursing home, where she shared a room with her partner of fifty-eight years. She had been attracted to women very early in her life, and for a long time she believed no others in the world were like her. Sent off to boarding school in her teens, she found her first partner there. Madelyn lived in a world of denial and blending. Her denial had been so complete and her blending so successful that she did not recall great concern about being "found out." In a tone of wonderment edged with regret, Madelyn described her life.

> [It] just seems like all my life, literally, I have lived and accepted, and everybody's accepted me. I haven't talked about it. . . . When I found partners, we never talked about it—ever. Blended in, never discussing anything. But we did all the things that normal people would do, and it was amazing, the way we were able to blend into everything. . . . We've [she and her current partner] been together very many years, and were able to live our lives perfectly normally. We did all that we wanted to do. We traveled. We never discussed this being gay. We never talked about it, even to this day. . . . She was on the same staff as I was and that's how we met. . . . They sent her all over the world, traveling. So a lot of our time together was correspondence, and then when she had vacations she'd come and always stay with me. . . . It's amazing, really, that all my life so much—I've never discussed it. It's a mistake to never discuss it. We lived this open life and never had any group experience with lesbians or anything like that. We just lived, blending into anything. Totally isolated, and didn't need anyone, we thought. Until I suddenly saw [at age ninety-four] that there were people out there and realized how completely repressed I was and didn't know it.

Considering the consequences of being known as lesbian during this time, it is not surprising that the women interviewed, especially those over sixty-five, demonstrated a singular lack of discussion of lesbianism. A code of silence prevailed. Although these women often did not question or wrestle with their sexual orientation, a few had lived most of their lives without discussing it, even with lesbian friends. Penny, age sixty-nine, maintained her silence until recently.

> I had a partner that I lived with for about fifteen years and . . . she and her friends and the people we knew together, we never discussed it. Never discussed it! And when I came up here and met some other lesbians, they could hardly believe that we never talked about it at all. I mean, with each other. Alone. In a room together. Or even in a bed. You didn't talk about it. . . .Well, I don't really know that I really ever said anything to anybody that I am gay or I am lesbian until I came up here. Until two years [ago]—now I am over sixty-nine—I never even referred to a lesbian or would I allow the word to pass my lips.

Penny's code of silence was influenced by the times, by her sense of privacy, and perhaps also by her previous five- or six-year involvement with a married woman. All provided good reasons for secrecy.

The military was another arena where the "code of silence" was critical. Discovery meant discharge. Elaine, now fifty-seven and very out, worked overseas for the military in a civilian capacity when she was in her twenties. She explained that she and her friends maintained the code of silence despite their established social network.

> And a bunch of us . . . that ran around together, we were all gay, but we never ever talked about it. You had your best friend that you traveled with. We would meet each other at conferences and conventions and workshops. We all hung together, but nobody ever talked about it.

Everyone worked hard to avoid acknowledging the obvious. This symbiosis, entered into by homosexuals and straight society alike, allowed the facade of uniformity to remain intact while obscuring the sexual underbelly. Similar to the broader society, biological family members often cooperated in maintaining silence by adopting a "don't ask, don't tell" approach. Many of the women believed their family members knew or at least suspected that they were lesbian. For some, this meant estrangement and avoidance. For others, families participated in the blending process by including partners in family gatherings and events but not acknowledging the nature of the relationship.

Barbara, age sixty-nine, believes her lifestyle is a private matter. Retired from teaching, she lives with her long-term partner, whom she described as being "comfortably out," at least in the lesbian community. Barbara described how their families treat their relationship.

> I don't know that I ever have [come out] to my family, although my family already—if they have their head outside of the sand—they recognize that I have been partners with women all my life. And some of them have even talked about the fact; they know, they recognize, and call my partner a member of the family as my partner's family calls me a cousin or a niece. And so I think they accept who we are for what we are. But it is not discussed, and I don't discuss it. I don't go out of my way to rub people's noses in my lifestyle; it is not necessary, as far as I am concerned.

Although blending provided a means for some women to appear to live a "normal" life, others found that being isolated from lesbian and gay contact was unacceptable. Instead, they chose to lead a double life. Similar to blending, it provided the appearance of being "normal," but it allowed participation in the underground gay life of the times.

Kay, age seventy-one, remained closeted because she believed her career in the mental health field would be hurt if her lesbianism were discovered. Her fear of being identified as a lesbian was so great that she dated men, rented office space to men only, always attended conferences with men, and took men with her when she visited her family during holidays. For years she and a gay male friend passed themselves off as engaged. She maintained a heterosexual facade as rigidly as she buried any association with lesbianism.

> [I was] absolutely closeted—totally. . . . I don't think I ever came out of the closet as a lesbian until I retired, which was about five years ago, because up until then I was very much in the closet all the time. Never went to any organizations, didn't join anything, didn't belong to anything where I could be identified as a lesbian. In fact I was kind of offended by the word. I didn't like to hear that word. I never went anywhere with women to anything, in town, where I lived. When I lived on the West Coast, I would go to San Francisco with a woman or

women. When I came here, I would go to San Francisco, I would go to Portland, or I would go to Seattle and go to gay places or be seen with lesbian women, but never here, where I lived. It was always a cover-up.

Eileen, now sixty-eight and retired from a nursing career, kept her lesbian relationships totally hidden. It was only when she moved to the Pacific Northwest from the Midwest that she began living a double life.

Out here I didn't say anything at work or anything, but we'd go to the Double Header and we'd go to the Mad—that club on Madison—and that was neat. But then as soon as we left [the bar], then that was the end of that kind of life. Go right back to the straight life. And the people I associated with at the bars and stuff were not the people I associated with when I wasn't there, and they didn't associate with me either. . . . Very separate, yeah. So it was almost like living two lives.

The stigma of being "abnormal" was so traumatic that even today many of the women are still unable to be comfortable in a more open society. For Margaret, age sixty-one, her years of working for small, individually owned, homophobic companies kept her firmly in the closet for safety reasons. After her retirement, she evolved an uneasy compromise: In a world increasingly open to the subject of homosexuality, she generally avoided any discussion of lesbian issues.

Well, it's been—in some ways, it's real uncomfortable because I'm not used to living openly in the gay world. I've always lived so closeted that it became such a way of life to me that I haven't experienced the freedom that I've heard other people talk about. I had a friend here over the weekend, an eighty-eight-year-old woman that I've known all my life, and she knows that I'm a lesbian—we've never discussed it. But she does antidiscrimination work . . . that involves gays and lesbians, and she spent the weekend talking about it, and I kept thinking, "Talk about something else," you know. So I'm not real comfortable with it in that respect.

GROWING UP DIFFERENT

A number of the women interviewed knew they were different from a very young age. A few even had a sense of what that difference might be. Kate, age sixty-one, knew that she liked girls, not boys, from about the age of six or eight. She also instinctively understood that she shouldn't talk about it. Fortunately, she found others like herself.

> I was an athlete when I was young and so I played lots of sports, particularly I played competitive softball and of course met a lot of other young lesbians, my age group. And we just sort of formed friendships and support groups and that kind of thing. I started playing competitive softball when I was thirteen years old and this continued for a lot of years. By the time I graduated from high school I knew, of course, I was a full-blown lesbian, and my mother, I'm sure, had inklings and was worried about me. But I always had this group of friends that were also lesbian who I ran around with and did things with.

Not all of the women were as lucky as Kate. Many of the women who experienced themselves as being different felt isolated, even if they had not identified their difference as one of sexual orientation.

Judy, age fifty-seven, grew up in the Midwest. Her father died when she was very young, leaving the family very poor. Although the overriding difficulties in her childhood were due to poverty, she also described coping with being different.

> Growing up was absolutely dreadful. I was very isolated. I think I was always different, I think I was always a lesbian. I think I was born one, but I didn't know that. . . . I was brighter than most of the kids, so my tendency in terms of being isolated was to attribute that to simply being brighter. . . . Although I knew I was a bit different and I knew I was isolated and I knew I was miserable . . . I did not feel that there was anything wrong with me.

The same age as Judy, Elaine grew up in a small town. Her early realization that she was gay and keeping that secret separated her from her friends.

I feel like I'm one of these folks, if there is such a thing, that knew from a very, very young age that I was somehow different, and at that point I didn't have words to put around it. I didn't know how to describe it. But it's sort of like I can remember high school, and this sounds very dramatic, but like I was looking through a glass window? I could see all of my friends but I really wasn't with them in a lot of different ways. I became kind of the class clown and got very involved in a lot of activities and was very popular, but I was real terrified that—I used to sneak into libraries and read about homosexuality, and back in that era it was not classy. It was classified as a disorder of some type.

Adolescence was a time when a number of the women became aware of their same-sex attractions. Most did not have the words to interpret their feelings or the information to give their experiences context and meaning. Like Elaine, they went looking for information.

Denise realized at the age of twelve that she might be homosexual when a neighbor told her about sex and explained what a homosexual was. She described her predicament as a teenager in the 1950s.

In high school, I did a long paper. It was part of my senior project—on homosexuality. And the stuff that was available—now I graduated in 1958, and the stuff that was available, at least that I got a hold of, was very psychiatric, very onus oriented, very negative. And I really did—I incorporated a lot of those views because those were the only views available. So it was a struggle.

Now sixty-three and retired from a teaching career, Maria's sense of being different resulted in a search for words to understand her feelings and experiences.

I was living in [a state in the South] at the time and I was thirteen, and [when] you're a teenager in [that state] that's when you start to date and the man next door said to me, "Well, you're going to be thirteen. Who are you going out on your first date with?" To which I responded, "Oh, I'm going to . . . take Marjorie to the movies." To which he replied, "What are you, a queer?" Well, I knew by his tone that something was amiss. So I immediately went into the house and asked my sister Janice,

"What's a queer?" She said, "Oh, honey, that's a word that people use when they're referring to homosexuals." Well, I didn't know what homosexual was either. So I went to the dictionary and that really wasn't much help, so then I went to the library and I finally found out that a homosexual is somebody who loves people of their same sex. And I said, "Yes, that's it. That's it."

Maria's family was unusually supportive of her sexuality. Her mother gave her advice about her love relationships, and one of her sisters took her to bars because she was too young to drive and to parties because she was too shy to go on her own. Later, her teaching career sent her into the closet, where she stayed until she was in her late forties.

Eleanor, age seventy-two, was not as fortunate as Maria in terms of family response. By the time she was eleven or twelve, Eleanor knew she was different and that her "life was going to be with another female." Although she was comfortable with her decision, she learned early that the less said the better, and that restrictions dictated how she should behave. When her family would not accept her lesbianism, she left home at age sixteen and got a job in a gay club in Greenwich Village. She spent five or six years "knocking around" in the Village and then moved to Long Island and began her business career. Although she remained out to family and friends, work required being in the closet.

All my life it's been pretty much the same. Primarily I've been in business for myself all my life and that keeps me closeted. And particularly my generation—it's probably a little bit different now. I don't know, but it feels different. Hell, when I was a kid, you wouldn't dare say the word "lesbian." I'm not sure I even knew how to spell it.

In spite of the pressure to hide their lesbianism, some of the women tried not to remain invisible. Unfortunately, parents and other family members often were instrumental in closing off the option of visibility. Many of the women who felt that they were different from an early age reported that they thought one of their parents, usually their mother, sensed something. Some mothers gave an indication that they knew, such as suggesting their daughter was "abnormal" without offering specifics. Most remained silent or approached the subject indirectly. For instance, Jennifer, age sixty, reflected upon a saying that her mother repeated frequently when Jennifer was young. It did not bring succor and reassurance.

> She used to say that old saying about everybody in the world is a little queer except for thee and me, and sometimes I think you're a little queer. Well, one day she changed that from queer to odd. And I had a feeling she knew then—that she knew for sure, emotionally. And I think that's probably before she intercepted some of my letters. And then when she did, she never said anything. She just said, "There's letters at the house for you."

Long before she ever thought that she might be lesbian, Betty, age sixty-five, asked her mother what a homosexual was. Her mother replied, "Well, men knock out their front teeth so they can have sex with a man." No more enlightened than she was before, Betty continued her search for an answer, which led her to the Bible, the Kinsey reports, and *The Well of Loneliness*. The latter especially left her with the belief that she could look forward only to a life of despair. Betty was among a number of women who sought to understand their feelings and experiences through any available literature, such as Hall's novel—the standard depiction of forbidden love. She described how the book left her with a sense of fear of her own fate.

> I remember reading *The Well of Loneliness,* and I thought, well, it really is kind of an iffy future if you're different. I called it just "homosexual." I didn't know what other name to call it. . . . Well, I thought, oh, if you are homosexual, then you're in for a life of despair. And that really wasn't a nice feeling.

After she graduated from college Betty got a job she loved with a youth organization. Knowing she would be fired if discovered, she spent years trying unsuccessfully to find men with whom she could fall in love. In the meantime, she found women. Eventually she gave up the idea of marrying but not her quest for normalcy. She hoped a psychiatrist could "cure" her, but that failed. It was not until she was almost forty years old that she acknowledged to herself that she was a lesbian.

Although she knew she was lesbian by the age of ten or twelve, Sylvia married at eighteen because she thought her attraction to women was just a phase. While she was in nurses' training, she read *The Well of Loneliness,* which put the "fear of God" in her. She married twice, divorced twice, and raised her children partly in the context of a closeted long-term lesbian relationship. She remained uncomfortable with unanswered questions.

> I knew I was different, but I can't say I always wanted to be. It bothered me and I wondered why. . . . I don't think one would ever choose to be because it's not the life that one chooses. You know, it's too hard. If I had my choice I wouldn't be gay. I'm not ashamed that I am, but I still would not choose it.

The "fear of God" inspired by *The Well of Loneliness* was not unique to Sylvia. A number of women experienced strong reactions to the book. Some credited it with sending them into denial to avoid the sad life it portrayed. Faced with a choice between living the American dream of being a wife and mother or the depressing lesbian life depicted in the literature of the day, it was no contest.

MARRIAGE AND MOTHERHOOD

The social imperative for women to marry was so strong that over half of the participants felt that the fulfillment of that expectation was their only option. Family and peer pressure led some women to the altar; others married to avoid being confronted about being gay or to prove their heterosexuality—even to themselves. Many women sought to repress their feelings or to escape the reality of their attractions by getting married.

While at college during the 1950s, Carolyn recognized her attraction to women and had an affair with her roommate, but she could not deal with the stigma.

> Actually, I'm one of those lesbians that had an affair with a woman when I was in college, with my college roommate—that was in the 1950s. That was not a good time to be gay because . . . it was unnatural, it was a sickness. There was great gay bashing;

it was considered to be an illness. And I didn't really know much about this except that I knew liking my college roommate wasn't what I was supposed to do, that it was not okay. So it was very closeted and I did get caught. . . . The woman I worked with read my mail and she confronted me with it, and she said that she would pay for me to see a shrink. To cure me. So, I didn't— so I just stopped. It was a bigger problem than I could handle. So then I just went about working on the American dream and got married and had a couple of kids.

Beth, who was fifty-five when she was interviewed, dated men and eventually married because of social pressures, not because it was something she wanted or even consciously decided.

I was deliberately blonde, blue-eyed, and tall, and in the 1950s that was standard. And so, because I was so attractive to men, that made me not realize that what counted is how I felt. But as girls then, you were the object, and so somehow my orientation was shaped by the fact that men were attracted to me. . . . I was fumbling and wondering and not sure what [was] going on in my life and I didn't particularly care for men. I just . . . went along with the relationships with them because that's what was done.

Some of the women deliberately maintained fictional marriage engagements in order to dispel any awareness that they were gay. Others saw marriage as the only way to fit in, "to be regular and normal and everything." This was the case for Donna, age seventy-one. Aware of her attraction to women in early adolescence, she felt very alone. Now a retired public school teacher, she remembered trying to find her way in isolation.

I had been attracted to women since I was twelve years old, but in the Midwest I didn't find anybody who had similar feelings and when I went to college . . . I decided I'd get married because I assumed it would be safer for an adult. . . . There wasn't anybody out there that would say, "well, you don't have to do that." I have friends now that never got married, but somehow or another they, seems to me, must have had some . . . support somewhere.

Looking back, Janet, now fifty-eight, reported that she knew she was gay at age six and had her first affair with a woman at age seventeen. Although she was involved with a married woman, she did what people did back then: She dated men in order to "put on a front . . . so nobody would know." However, when she became pregnant, she married the father to provide a name for her child.

> When I was married, it was hell. It was pure hell. But I got pregnant and I was going to have my baby. I was going to give her a name. . . . It was the worst three years of my life, being married. But I got a beautiful daughter out of it, and that was important. I would never give up that . . . she's probably the most important thing in my life.

In her twenties, Claudia, age seventy-four, spent time at a San Francisco lesbian bar, where she watched the women and noticed how unhappy they looked. She decided that life was going to be hard enough without living as a lesbian, so despite her attractions to women, she did what was expected: She married a man. Later she turned to alcohol.

> I was drawn like a magnet to women that were gay. . . . [I was] wide-eyed and fascinated but kind of scared. You know, scared. . . . Anyway, I had this terrific crush on this gal when I was in the [military], but I steered clear of her. It was just like, ooh, I got this crush—she never knew it. . . . I kept [it] all within myself . . . and after I was discharged, I married again. I married a man. . . . I led the suburban housewifey thing, in the 1950s and 1960s. But I was never happy; I was always miserable. I was miserable in my marriage, I was miserable within myself, and I started drinking. And I drank, and I didn't like it—I mean, I didn't like myself, but I did it anyway.

Other women also paid the price, "doing the right thing" by marrying or staying married. Christine, age sixty-four, is a recovering alcoholic who lives in a small town on the coast and recently moved in with her new partner. Looking back on her life, she believes she was always a lesbian, but she first fell in love with a woman after she had been married for ten years and had three children. Although he didn't understand her lesbianism, her husband was very supportive and accepting.

> Because we were not miserable together, we decided to wait
> for—until the kids were old enough and we felt they could tolerate our being separated. And so we stayed together five more
> years and it was a terrible period for me. I was just turned upside
> down and inside out. I was plagued with guilt for being a lesbian
> when everyone around me was not.

Still others married because they wanted to have children. Pat, age sixty-nine, married on the rebound after her lesbian partner left her. Marriage seemed like the only alternative, especially since she wanted to have children.

> I'd been with a woman for six years; we were going to spend our
> life together. She met a guy coming out of the service—that was
> right after World War II. She met a guy, fell in love with him,
> and I was up the creek, brokenhearted . . . and I went the wrong
> way. I went into marriage. What were the alternatives? She and I
> were together, but there wasn't any community. There weren't
> any bars. We didn't know another lesbian couple. There were
> some gay bars, but they were all [for] men. And when she left
> me, I had nothing. I didn't have anyone to talk to about it. . . .
> I didn't see an alternative except to marry. . . . And I remember
> when I realized I was gay, there was a certain disappointment
> there for me because I thought I wouldn't have children. In
> those days they didn't have baster babies. It wasn't done. . . .
> I had never really accepted the idea of not having children, and I
> know I married on the rebound. I liked him. I knew he would be
> a good husband and father. I was not in love with him.

After many years of marriage, when her three children were grown, Pat realized she wanted out. However, it was not easy to leave her marriage.

> I was in a dependent state, which happens to women who stay
> home and don't work, raise the kids. I was married for twenty-four years and you get into one thing. I went back to college as a
> freshman when I was forty-eight years old because I was so

damned scared of divorce. . . . There were no displaced home-maker programs then . . . so I was kind of doing my own program.

RESISTANCE AND REBELS

A few women, with a strong source of strength to be themselves, rebelled at the then-prevalent belief that all women had to marry and raise a family. As a young adult, Frances found the strength to break off her engagement. At fifty-five, she considered that time—when she decided who she would be—one of the best moments in her life.

I think one of the most remarkable times in my life is when I decided that I didn't want to be married, that I wanted to be a lesbian. I was twenty-one years old. And I just—I said to myself, "You have a choice in your life. Either you get married and do what everybody thinks you should, or do what you want to do. So, what do you want to do? How would you be happiest?" And I decided I'd be the happiest not married.

Amy, age sixty-two at the time of her interview, never considered marriage or the closet an appealing option. Coming of age in the early 1950s, she may well represent an incipient movement questioning the shame, fear, internalized hatred, and the lesbian orthodoxy of butch/femme roles characteristic of those who came of age in earlier eras.

I have never been in the closet; I came out when I was nineteen and stayed out. And [I've] never been a closet believer, and was one of those people in the trenches fighting for rights when it was unpopular. . . . When I finally figured it out, which took a while because in my day there was no literature, there was no support group. In fact, everything was underground. And particularly since there were bars where you really should have been twenty-one. To me the biggest hurdle was telling my parents, and they're the first ones I told. My father [dealt with it] by taking a bath, and my mother cried. . . . I was one of the women in the [early days] and one of the things we really struggle[d] with was what role we were supposed to have, and there was an awful lot of copying heterosexual couples, which always seemed ridiculous to me, even way back then. I can remember very clearly women going to bars in sports coats and ties, and you know, somebody five-foot-two looked pretty much like a jerk. It wasn't something I did. . . . I had a real difference in philosophy with the way [other lesbians] saw it. They were into [butch/femme] roles. I mean, if you went to their house for dinner, if you were the butchy one, you went out and saw the tools, and if you weren't, you stayed in the house and did whatever you did in the house. It was a real dichotomy and I thought, my God, we're all women; isn't that the point?

Joan explained that she had married at sixteen only to realize later that she was attracted to women. Once she recognized her sexual orientation, Joan refused to be in the closet—at home, at work, or even when it involved the potential loss of custody of her daughter.

I realized that as much as you want to do the right thing, you just say, "Hey, look, we only go around life one time." So what I did is I took my daughter and I left. So when I finally came back home . . . [my husband] wanted the custody of my daughter, claiming desertion. . . . He knew at that point that I was a homosexual and of course he went to his attorney and said, "Well, I want custody because of desertion, because my wife is a homosexual." Well, so, naturally I wasn't going to give, wasn't going to just say, "Well, yeah, sure, here."

Eventually, Joan did get legal custody of her daughter.

COMING OUT OLDER

Some women did not face the question of whether to come out early in life because they did not recognize that they were indeed lesbian until midlife or beyond. For example, Catherine, now sixty-three, never wanted to be the traditional housewife or even to get married. At nineteen she entered a convent but left after two months because she found the discipline intolerable. A few years later she became pregnant and then married. Over time she raised five children, divorced her husband, earned a university degree, and at age fifty-nine realized that she was a lesbian. The one thing she would most like to have now is "an old Boston marriage."

A number of the women socialized with lesbians but never imagined that they had the same proclivities. Paula, age sixty-six, commented, "I was aware that there were lesbians. And I had some social contact, and you know it was no big deal—it didn't matter. But it never occurred to me that that's who I was." Betty, age sixty-five, explained, "I didn't think I was gay. I just hung out with all these people who were gay."

Edith, age seventy-one, did not recognize what was missing from her life until she had a "midlife crisis."

> I didn't [come out] until I was fifty-five. The result was a feeling of completion that—something that had always been sort of a niggling thorn was finally resolved and removed. I married and had children. But I got to the point, I suppose midlife crisis, one of those catch-all phrases, there's something missing. . . . Fortunately, my children were married or gone so I didn't have that child custody or anything like that to battle. I said, "I'm moving out." . . . My husband's response was, "Oh, I guess we'll have to sell the house."

Muriel, age fifty-eight, described what it was like when she became aware of her feelings for another woman.

> I had been married for thirteen years, had three children, and so it was very, very upsetting to realize that I was gay after this amount of time. And at the time, my husband and I had been in counseling. . . . It was very traumatic. . . . We were neighbors, visiting back and forth, that type of thing. Sally and I seemed to have a lot more in common. Bob [my husband] and Sally's husband would sit in the room and visit and [talk of] building stuff, things of that nature, and Sally and I'd sit at the other end and visit about things that were important. We just kept seeing more—I found lots of excuses to go and visit, that type of thing. I [asked her], "Do you feel the same way I feel toward you?" And she kind of stumbled and sputtered and didn't answer. It wasn't until I went home, played back that question that I realized what I had said and what it meant to me. So, that's kind of how it evolved.

Once the realization had surfaced, Muriel divorced her husband, and Sally moved in with Muriel and her three children. They lived a closeted life and were acquainted with no other lesbians. Only within the last few years have they had any contact with the lesbian community.

Jill, fifty-five years old when she was interviewed, had been out for eight years. When she admitted to herself that she was lesbian, she felt disoriented.

> It's like a whole change of my identity. . . . It's like all of a sudden here I am, forty-plus years old, and I don't know who the hell I am. . . . It was sort of like, "Who am I? What is going on?" I'm no longer any of the things that I thought I was . . . I'm just discovering me. It's like my understanding of what happened to me as a child and as a woman in the 1950s—it just kept me frozen.

Seventy-four years old at the time of her interview, Claudia recalled how her awakening almost resulted in tragedy.

> I was utterly miserable. I was in this heterosexual marriage. I had these kids. I was living in [California] and suddenly I'm forty. And I just thought, God, you know that old cliché, life begins at forty? And I felt like I was a hundred and ninety years old and in some terrible trap; and I was drinking too much and I didn't like myself. Oh, I didn't like the things I was doing, but I was doing them anyway. When I drank I got mouthy with people. . . . Anyway, I tried to kill myself. I took a whole bottle of Valium and I drank a whole bunch of booze and I went to bed to end it all. It didn't work. It's a wonder I'm not brain damaged or some horrible thing. . . . But you know, I felt free. I know who I am. I suffered for so many years in this damn denial thing.

Eventually Claudia found her way to recovery in Alcoholics Anonymous (AA) and began a process of self-acceptance. During her recovery she fell in love with a woman, but she still could not completely accept herself and the relationship ended. She continued to socialize primarily with lesbians in AA but remained in denial about herself. It was not until she was in her sixties and retired that she concluded that she was a lesbian. Subsequently a friend told her about a meeting of older lesbians. She felt at home in that group and has been open ever since about her sexual orientation.

Almost twenty years younger than Claudia, Stephanie came out at about the same age, but their experiences differed significantly. Stephanie credits her father for encouraging her to be independent and to pursue her desires. When she recognized that she was lesbian, she left a flourishing law practice and headed west.

> I came out to myself by falling in love with a woman when I was thirty-eight; my friends knew about it before I did. I was married, had a child, and just, you know, slipped into falling head over heels in love with this woman, and this was back [on the East Coast]. . . . My husband and I were very close, great companions. We worked together sometimes, we jogged together, we were best friends, the whole nine yards. But when I became so enchanted with this woman—what I described was that it felt like I had been dying a little bit around the edges and all of a sudden there was new life. So that I think that was the more compelling emotional response than fear or whatever about, "My God, am I queer?" I had those questions and I also had my good friend and law partner who had been in a relationship with a woman for a few years. And so we had each other to talk to, nobody else. . . . We became involved in the Women Attorneys Association, quite active in it, and through that began to kind of surreptitiously meet other lesbians. But a big deal wasn't made of it. We just kind of gravitated. And then coming out to [the west] was—coming alive. And so here I have nothing to lose and everything to gain, and it just now feels like I'm a lesbian, just like I'm white and in my fifties and it's an important part of me, but most of the time it doesn't have any charge of fear or discomfiture or concern about what somebody will think of me. I'm just open. And it is wonderful.

Like Stephanie, a number of the women discovered their lesbianism through a relationship with a particular woman. That was the situation for Evelyn, age fifty-five. From an "all-Catholic background" in the Midwest, she joined the military after high school because her father believed the state university was full of communists so she shouldn't attend. During her military service, she was surprised to find herself kissed by another woman from her baseball team.

I was in Sue's room one night . . . and she leaned over and she
kissed me. "Why'd you do that?" "Because I like to!" I said,
"Oh." And she said, "What do you think?" I said, "I don't know.
I'll get back to you later. I'll think about it." So I got up and left. I
went out to this huge oak tree we had. I'll never forget it. Pretty
soon she comes wandering out. She says, "Are you okay?" And
I said, "Yeah." And she said, "Did I offend you?" And I said,
"No, I don't think so." And she says, "Well, I didn't mean to."
She said, "You know, I really wanted to do that." So I said,
"Okay." She says, "Well, I'm going back in." . . . So, anyhow, I
went wandering back in a little while later . . . and I said, "Can
we do that again?"

Among those interviewed, Paula's experience was unique. Now
sixty-six, Paula met a group of lesbians through her daughter. After
twenty-eight years of marriage, her association with these young
women provided the impetus for her to explore her own sexuality.

My oldest daughter was about nineteen and she was going to
school and working and she belonged to an all-women's bowling team from work. She said, "Can I bring my friends home?"
Thursday night was open house. My children, teenagers, could
bring their friends in and it was spaghetti night. We'd just throw
an extra handful of spaghetti in. So she says, "Can I bring my
friends from the bowling team?" I said, "Sure." And they walked
in the door and I knew they were lesbians! I just knew. . . . So she
brings these women home and we eat and the kids went and did
their homework and I'm alone at the kitchen table with these
women. We just talked up a storm and they kind of told me their
stories. Every one of them had been molested or beat up by a
brother or father or something. Oh, I just wanted to console
them because I'm a mother and I'm older than them. And they
wound up calling me Mom and I still keep in touch with a couple [of them] to this day. They were wonderful—I loved it. And
then they took me to a bar and I danced with them and everything. It was wonderful; it was such a freedom. . . . That's when
my self-image really started. That's when I started to feel who I
was, feel my own power as a woman and as a person.

THE MOVEMENTS

The gay liberation movement, the women's movement, feminism, and the political activism of these movements were not prominent factors in most of the women's decisions to be closeted or not. The American Psychiatric Association's depathologizing of homosexuality by removing it from the *Diagnostic and Statistical Manual of Mental Disorders* in 1973 also did not play a direct role. More important factors in coming out included chronological age and the experience of being lesbian. In general, the oldest women experienced the most severe social negativity and oppression. These women tended to feel that the movements did not speak to them—that they came too late. Some mentioned the magazines, bookstores, choruses, and concerts as positive outcomes. But even those who acknowledged the beneficial effects did not feel that the movements impacted them significantly. As one woman stated, "Well, I think the gay liberation movement has not impacted me personally, and yet if it weren't for that, the women I have met here would not have been in the least out and I never would have met them."

Many of the women interviewed could not easily accept the growing openness. In her mid-sixties, Teresa's discomfort with gay liberation was not uncommon for women her age. "I think some folks go too far, you know—the Pride Day, for example. I'm uncomfortable with some of it, but that's just me." Mary Alice, age sixty-eight, equivocated about the overall effects of the various civil rights/liberation movements in general and feared a possible backlash.

> [I'm] very ambivalent. I have a lot of anger about it and some degree of gratitude that the movement started with as much fervor as it has. I'm not—I struggle with myself about advocacy. I think I object to the ways in which heavy-handedness of the movement has been portrayed or done. . . . I fear that [with] all of these breast-beating and tugging about that groups are doing, homosexuality is going to [go] like the women's movement in general and the black movement, civil rights movement in general seems to have gone: the pendulum all the way left and then back all the way right.

Many of the women, like seventy-two-year-old Eleanor, were supportive from a distance but could not themselves assume a more out and active way of life.

> I have not been as active as I would, in my heart, have liked to have been. Growing up during the Depression, making a living was always a big thing in my life. I just didn't want to mess with my livelihood so I was covertly supportive.

Gay pride events made Eileen, age sixty-eight, feel that she was on the outside looking in at something very different from her experience.

> I remember the first Gay Pride parade I went to. I couldn't believe it. Here all these lesbians and gays there marching in front of God and everybody with their signs and banners. I thought— I almost cried . . . it was so foreign to us to see. It was just marvelous that here they could express themselves, and I just still felt like a person watching.

In general, the younger women tended to be more open and out. The support they'd experienced from various gay, lesbian, and/or feminist groups helped them to be out successfully at work or in public. For example, Susan became aware that she was lesbian during her midthirties, when she was married and ostensibly straight. Two years after that, with support from the women's movement in the early 1970s, she acknowledged that her marriage was over and came out as a lesbian.

> [With] massive support all around me, even in the National Organization [for] Women [NOW], which is where I started out, the maxim was, "Never let a man come between two sisters"; even if you were heterosexual, that was dogma. . . . There was tremendous support . . . so I never went through some of the bad old times that people in earlier decades had to go through about being—their jobs were at risk or their families were at risk or whatever. Or that they might get beaten up in bars or anything like that.

When women did identify some impact of the gay rights movement, it ranged from general to powerfully specific. Those who acknowledged a general effect thought the movement made being lesbian "a lot easier than it had been before." A few mentioned the sense of strength in numbers and believed the movement has helped people realize how many gays and lesbians exist. Although putting a human face on homosexuality has opened up dialogue, many women emphasized that coming out was still "a very frightening thing to do." As Jane, age fifty-nine, put it, "Even though the movement has given me the willingness to quietly be able to say to people that don't really know that, well, I'm a gay woman. . . . I think it's me taking the risk all the time."

Some women felt that their lives had been strongly affected by the political movements of the 1970s. Catherine, now sixty-three, was living in Montana when she heard Sonia Johnson, a lesbian separatist, speak. "My reaction was, I would follow that woman anyplace. I was so impressed with her." For Susan, age fifty-six, coming out publicly was an easy step to take because of the "massive support" she experienced in the women's movement. Other women mentioned that in going to a women's center or lesbian center or getting involved in organizing in the lesbian community, they found a new sense of freedom and capacity to be themselves. A former journalist—among other occupations— and now retired, Audrey's experience was typical.

> The lesbian/gay rights movement in [a West Coast city], which had been going on for a while—far more, I assure you, than in [another state]—did indeed make a difference in my life. . . . I changed my name back to my maiden name and determined that whomever I was talking with would know the truth. I never hid my lesbian-ness once I was over here. It enabled me to be myself and put away all pretenses.

Maria had an epiphany after the death of her sister, which spurred her to move out from behind the scenes in her political involvement in the early 1980s.

> I stayed in the closet until about fifteen years ago, when my younger sister died and it all of a sudden dawned on me that I could die, and nobody would know who the hell I was. And then I decided to come out. I wanted gay friends and to be involved.

My lover at the time said "No way," so we parted and I started joining groups. I had been paying dues but now I started going to meetings—went to the local NOW meeting and joined the Lesbian Rights Task Force.

Of all the women interviewed, the gay pride movement impacted Madelyn most powerfully. Now age ninety-five, she was only recently able to talk openly about her life for the first time.

The parades and the fact that there were organizations and that people were talking about it finally—that did tremendous things for me. It sort of brought me out of something. I don't know, but suddenly I felt free. I could talk about it.

Chapter 2

Identity

I have likened it to the fitting of cogs in a template of some sort, where they fit all right in the original position, but that shift— even though it seemed a pretty small shift at the time—just made it fit properly.

Edith, age seventy-one

How we define ourselves is primary to the experiences we have throughout life. Identity helps us to develop our sense of self, our confidence as well as our doubts, and guides us on our journey through time. Few of the women interviewed had a name for what they felt growing up. Often they had no one to talk to and no positive images of lesbians or a lesbian "lifestyle." In this context, an examination of language is instructive because it reflects the changes over time in how society views lesbians as well as how they describe themselves. Throughout the 1950s, "homosexual" was the primary term used by the media to describe both men and women. In keeping with the times, it had a clinical—not to mention judgmental—ring to it. Clearly the major characteristic of "those people" was sexual behavior, and homosexuality was perceived as sick and distasteful. Then in the 1960s, Del Martin and Phyllis Lyon's groundbreaking book, *Lesbian/Woman,* reclaimed the term lesbian from the clutches of exclusively pejorative use. Over the years, lesbians' self-descriptions have ranged from "that way," to "homosexual," "gay," "lesbian" (and more recently "dyke" and "queer"), with women choosing the term that was most compatible, depending upon their particular experiences and their historical context.

Sexual orientation was an important component of identity for the women interviewed—but not the only one. In this chapter we address the broad and complex topics of self-definition and identity. Asking these older lesbians how they identify themselves, what shaped and influenced their development, and what gives meaning to their lives invited them to further address these topics. We explore the events, experiences, and important influences that contributed to the participants' sense of who they are. This includes the time and place in which the women came of age, their families, and society at large, all of which played instrumental roles in the women's development of their sense of self. In addition, the women shared how critical turning points and their spiritual beliefs shaped the meaning and the essence of their lives.

WHAT'S IN A NAME?

How do older lesbians describe themselves? Among the women interviewed, it seems to depend in large part on chronological age and on the tenor of the times in which a woman first self-identified as lesbian. For various reasons, a majority of the women interviewed preferred the term "gay" to "lesbian."

Ellen, age sixty-two when she was interviewed, grew up in the 1950s and was very affected by the negative view of homosexuals in that era. She had "little liaisons" beginning in the seventh grade and, believing that something was wrong with her, kept them a secret. She tried to be "normal" by periodically swearing off women and even getting married.

> I guess it's the growing up and hearing that word ["lesbian"] and people were so cruel with it. . . . It just got planted in me—the seed—so early on that I really don't like it. So I like "gay." I'm just more comfortable with it.

Denise was fifty-seven at the time of her interview. She was aware of her same-sex attractions when she was young and recalls internalizing the negative views about homosexuality because they were the only ones available in the 1950s. She acknowledges that coming to terms with her sexual orientation has been a struggle and prefers the term "gay" to describe her orientation. "I have always thought of myself as a gay woman. I like the adjective—I prefer an adjective to describe myself rather than a noun."

The women who came out in the context of the women's movement, during which the term "lesbian" was reclaimed, typically identified themselves as lesbian. However, a few of the women identified
as lesbian long before the term was fashionable. Now seventy, Joan
responded enthusiastically to the question of how she identifies herself.

> I think of myself as an honest, straightforward lesbian. Always
> have been, always will be. The only difference between me and
> anybody else is that I just happen to like sleeping with a woman.
> The rest is all the same. You got to work, eat, sleep, get up in the
> morning, pay bills . . .

Others have used different terms interchangeably or have shifted
their terminology over time. Some used the term "gay" until "the men
took it over." Many mentioned that they found the term "lesbian" easier to use as its negative connotations lessened. Barbara, age sixty-
nine, captured the personal experience of the changing times. "I'm
from the period where it was 'homosexual.' . . . [Now] gay probably
would come out first, then I'd correct it and say lesbian."

A number of women were careful to point out that they did not
identify themselves primarily in terms of their sexual orientation. For
some their ethnic identity was primary. Other ways they identified included "woman," "feminist," "recovering Catholic," and "Democrat." A few emphasized their spiritual nature—one woman called
herself "a child of God"—while others identified as "just me—the
human being," or simply said, "I just am."

Grace, age seventy, identifies as "a human being first . . . as a spiritual being." A first-generation American, Grace married at the age of
twenty-four to get away from home. Three and a half years later, her
husband—who had been bisexual—died. About a year after his
death, she started going to a gay bar he had introduced her to, where
she just sat and watched people. She moved to California after her
sister "outed" her to their parents and they disowned her. Ultimately
she realized she was a lesbian and lived in partnered relationships.
Celibate for many years now, Grace described herself as "not a heterosexual or a homosexual; I'm sort of like in limbo." Her church af-
filiations and spiritual studies have been important throughout her
adult life, and she is currently involved in community work. "I guess

a lot of my life isn't about my being gay; it's about being a human because that's what I am first."

After marrying, having children, and caring for foster children, Mary had her first date with a woman when she was thirty-nine years old. Now fifty-five, she describes herself as a lesbian, but her racial and ethnic identity is primary to her.

> I don't think of myself as a lesbian first, though. I think of myself as a Native American woman who happens to be lesbian. And that's important to me because my basic identity is not so much lesbian; I just happen to be that. I happen to have diabetes. These are all tangential things in a way. Well, they're not tangential . . . but they're more additions to who I am rather than my basic identity. Being a Native American woman, that's my personal identity.

Clearly, for Grace and Mary, sexual orientation is not the primary component of their personal identity. For other women, their self-definition and identity has changed over time. Ellen, age sixty-two, was closeted for many years and came out in her fifties. She had gone to see a psychologist to deal with getting out of a lesbian relationship and thought, "While I'm here, maybe I can get over this stuff (i.e., being gay)." However, the opposite occurred. The psychologist told her she wasn't sick, and Ellen began accepting her sexual orientation. Now she describes being gay as "just a part of the overall me," but for most of her life it was a huge issue. "I think the secret is so big in your—being a secret, it takes up such a large part of you, you think that's all you are and you kind of lose the rest."

IDENTITY DEVELOPMENT

The quest for identity and the answer to the question, "Who am I?" is part of the developmental process for everyone. Factors such as the historical times, ethnicity, family influences, geographical location, and life experiences as well as temperament and personality all contribute to the uniqueness of each person's identity journey. For sexual minorities, sexual orientation is at least part of the equation. For those who deviate from the heterosexual path, the journey to a clear sense of self often takes particular twists and turns.

Convinced that she was not really homosexual, Carol, age seventy-four, spent a sizeable portion of her adult life trying to change before she finally accepted being a lesbian as part of her identity. Her process was similar to that of many other older lesbians.

> I think I grew up not really knowing who I was and, I think, probably fighting all of my life trying to find out who I was. And, in the interim, I fabricated all kinds of people to be, and none of the fabrications fit. So I was a lot of different people.

Many of the women shared Carol's experience of being different people. Sometimes this meant being one person privately and another publicly. Often it meant that identity evolved over time. Many of the women knew at an early age that they were different, whether or not they labeled it. Some even recognized this difference as one of sexual orientation. Others knew but suppressed their inclinations, led a secret life, or fled into the respectability—and safety—of marriage. Because these women grew up in a society that restricted women's identity to that of wife and mother and stigmatized homosexuality, only a very few of them were able to claim a lesbian identity at a young age.

Susan was fifty-six years old at the time of the interview. She had been married, in her early thirties, and very involved in the women's movement when she began her two-year process of identifying as a lesbian.

> It was like when I quit smoking, I became a nonsmoker in my head while I was still puffing cigarettes. And probably a year or so went by while I was still actually smoking, but I thought of myself as a nonsmoker before I actually quit. . . . I continued to be married and having sexual relationships [with men] where I thought of myself in my head as a lesbian.

A number of the women had a lesbian experience early in life and then changed direction. The discovery of her affair with a college roommate drove Carolyn, age fifty-seven, into heterosexuality. Many years later, after a divorce and while she was working in Europe, Carolyn began to explore her sexual orientation. One of her co-workers, a gay man, introduced her to the gay/lesbian world—bookstores, information about women's groups, and bars. Frustrated by going to a women's bar where she didn't speak the language and afraid to make contacts on the military base, she read books about the history of women and lesbians and tried to "catch up on thirty years of not doing what I should have been." Although she was never involved in a relationship in Europe, stepping into her lesbian identity was a very positive experience.

> I kind of blossomed there. I figured out my sexuality and I felt better about myself because of that. I'm more comfortable with myself. . . . From that point on, that's when I found myself and blossomed and I'm more relaxed and just a better person.

After returning to the United States, however, she faced the challenge of dating and the lack of confidence that accompanied being an older lesbian with no experience being with a woman.

> So I have to learn to date now, and over fifty. . . . It's like you have no experience, you know. You talk to a woman in her thirties and she thinks you're an older dyke. And she knows more than you do, and you have to tell her you just *look* like an old [i.e., experienced] dyke.

Almost twenty years older than Carolyn, Donna had an evolution that was markedly parallel—early awareness followed by fear and retreat into a more conventional, safer life. Donna recalled that she had been attracted to women since she was twelve years old, but in the Midwest she found no one with similar feelings. She described going to college.

> It was after World War II and that's what you do. You go to college and you find a man because if you don't find a man there, you're going to be lost. . . . [In college,] I was brought into the dean's office and given a talking to about any behavior that anybody might have reported. So I guess about that time I decided to get married because I assumed it would be safer for an adult.

For twenty-five years she dedicated herself to her family, followed her husband on various moves and unsuccessful ventures, all the while being aware of her attraction to women. Eventually Donna realized that she was trying to make the marriage work but that her husband was not. At that point she took charge of her life and made some decisions—to get a divorce and stay in the house to raise the kids. She credited therapy and the women's movement with helping her grow stronger and providing the support she needed to make these changes. Another factor was falling in love with a woman.

> I think it had to do with my relationship with another woman that was finally one of the first ones that really worked. I had had other relationships but this one really got to me. . . . It was probably the first time in my whole life I ever had been so touched and moved. . . . That experience opened up a whole area that I had never felt before. Ever. And then I just kind of went, "Oh, wow, life can be different. Life can be alive; you can burn with a hard, gemlike flame."

In describing her journey of self-development, Donna reflected on the time when she realized that she couldn't make yet another move with her husband.

> That was my first indication that wow, I had to give up me, had to give me up. I was swallowed in his life. I was swallowed. I was not me. And interestingly enough, when I decided I didn't want to be in this place anymore, I thought of myself as a person with a little flower growing out of the top of her head. I didn't want anyone to trample it. . . . There was something growing there that was going to be—have a name on it, and it might be "Donna." It might be.

Audrey, age sixty-three, is now retired from private practice as a therapist. She and her partner of eleven years share a love of exploring the Pacific Northwest. Audrey described her identity as a mosaic that developed through living a series of different lives, "so who I am now is sort of an eclectic experience." After college, she pursued a successful career in journalism and then married a man who turned out to be alcoholic.

> Talk about blind idiocy. I had no idea he was an alcoholic; neither of us had any idea that I was a lesbian, so you can imagine how well that worked out. Four years it lasted but it gave me two wonderful daughters and they shaped my life for the next eighteen years.

She had custody of her children but lived in fear that she could lose them—that the courts in her state would see her actively alcoholic husband as the better parent. To protect herself from losing her children—and from losing her job—she and her partner were very closeted and did not acknowledge their relationship to anyone, including the children.

During the back-to-the-land period in the 1960s, Audrey and her partner bought land and built up a farm. It was very hard work but everybody, including the kids, worked together, and they had fun. Eventually she tired of her job, and started her own remodeling business, where she could do something hands-on, creative, and solitary. After a few years of being her own boss, her relationship of fifteen years fell apart and she changed course again at the age of fifty. Audrey felt she had to explain what was going on to her mother, who was visiting for the Christmas holidays right in the middle of the breakup. Her mother reacted better than Audrey had feared—not accepting but at least tolerant. Deciding that she needed to start over somewhere else, Audrey moved to another city, started school to become a therapist, changed her name back to her maiden name, and decided not to hide anymore.

> Whomever I was talking with would know the truth. I never hid my lesbianism once I was over here. So it enabled me—actually that breakup was probably a terrific beginning. It enabled me to be myself and to put away all pretenses and clarify for myself. I felt like I was starting my life over.

Given the times when these women were growing up and coming of age, internalized homophobia colored their identity development. Most of the women spent at least some of their lives in the closet. A notable exception was Amy, now sixty-two, who described herself as a lesbian who has never been in the closet.

> When I was going to high school, I was a very popular kid. And I really kind of knew even then that I was different, but I didn't even know what the word was, you know? Some people say I don't want to be labeled—well, hell, I didn't even know what the labels were! I would have been glad to embrace one, I'm sure, but I didn't even know what they were. But I was a very popular kid and never had life experiences as I was growing up

... where I was isolated or shunned or picked on or any of those things.

She came out when she was nineteen and stayed out. Those first few years were difficult as she struggled on her own with figuring out her sexuality and reconciling that with her religious upbringing.

I was a Catholic in the age of sin and guilt. . . . Unfortunately, when you're nineteen years old, you don't have any frames of reference to even help yourself out and there was nobody to go to—that was kind of a tough time. I kind of just had to figure it out all by myself and I think my first reaction to that was to be defiant and just tell everybody with a chip on my shoulder. Unfortunately I did go through that, but I think that was a very tough time.

She was never ostracized by her parents or her extended family, never experienced "horrible hardships," and never lost a job because of her sexual orientation. Her identity as a lesbian continues to be central to her, so much so that she and her partner contribute financially to lesbian causes only.

FAMILY INFLUENCE ON IDENTITY

When asked to describe the events and experiences that shaped their lives and contributed to who they are, many women mentioned the influence of specific people in their lives, particularly family members. For some it was a parent or grandparent while for others it was siblings or their extended family of aunts, uncles, and cousins who exerted the strongest influence. Ann, age seventy-one, described her parents as very understanding and welcoming people who contributed greatly to her self-acceptance.

On weekends everybody liked to come over to our place because my mother fixed these big huge things that she'd put in the kitchen and everybody could eat, and my dad played the piano and sang crazy songs. So our house was sort of a focal point for our friends.

Ann's parents never pressured her to marry. They accepted who she was without any discussion. When she fell in love with a woman and began to spend most of her time with her, Ann's mother made a suggestion.

> "It's really crazy for [your friend] to keep paying rent on her place and the two of you are either here or over there. Why don't you see if she wouldn't like to just come here and live with you?" Because I was living at home. And I said, "Really?" And so my mother and dad thought this was just great. They loved her and she became just like another daughter to them, and she lived with us and we all had good times together.

Sharon's description of her growing-up years provides a sharp contrast to Ann's steadfastly warm and supportive family. Her mother died when she was born and she lived with her paternal grandparents on a ranch. Her father lived there as well but commuted to work in a city, so Sharon felt as if her grandfather raised her. Now fifty-nine years old, she recalls experiencing a great deal of loss at an early age. When she was twelve, her grandfather died, as did her dog, and when her grandmother moved out of the area, Sharon left the ranch and life she loved to live with her father in the city.

Her relationship with her father has always been strained. Although he never cut off contact completely, he "disowned" her for marrying a Catholic and then "disowned" her again, fourteen years later, for leaving her husband to be with a woman. However, she still loves him and acknowledges his influence in her becoming a self-sufficient and independent person.

> I've never been a big fan of my father, but the one thing he did— he was not a sexist. . . . And he raised us [she and her sister] to be independent and stand on our own two feet, to be able to support ourselves and not ever to have to depend on anybody to take care of us. And that's what got me through.

Laura, age fifty-seven, is a native Californian. Her grandfather settled in the state at the turn of the century—one of the first black families in the area. Her extended family had a great impact on her sense of herself.

I knew that I was special and I've always known that I was special. . . . Most of my cousins were ten to about fifteen years old when I was born. They would treat me like I was a little doll all the time and take me places, and that had a real impact on me because they would let me know that I could do anything. I could be anything I wanted to be and I didn't have to worry about other people, and they were there as members of my family. In retrospect, I think that really helped shape me, started the shaping for who I really am and what I really am, because I knew I was special. And they kept that up to this day, the cousins that I have, that shaped me, will tell me things that I did during that period. I was a very precocious child and they would show me off to their friends. . . . And they'd tell me various things I used to do which always made me feel as if they were very proud of me. . . . I never felt that I couldn't do something. Never. And I think it all stemmed from that early time in my life.

Family influenced the development of identity in yet another way. A number of the women interviewed mentioned specific advice they had been given while they were growing up. They took this advice to heart and shaped their lives based on it.

Although Penny's mother was a practicing alcoholic and the source of a good deal of unhappiness for her at a young age, Penny, now sixty-nine, also described her mother as "a very important mentor in my life."

One of the best pieces of advice I ever had, she gave me. I was very kind of inclined to go my own way and look like my own self, you know. So she said, "Look, it doesn't matter much what you think or what you are (this was not in reference to being a homosexual). It doesn't matter what you think inside and what you are inside, but you will find that you'll get along much better in the world if you appear to conform." And that really is pretty much the way I live. Because I do believe that you're better off to conform.

Maria, age sixty-three, provides another example of advice incorporated as a key aspect of personal identity. As the youngest child, she was raised primarily by her sisters. The age difference between her and her oldest sister was twenty years and she was "kind of handed down" from one sister to another. As one got married and left home, another took over. She described her experience as being the first child of each of her sisters and their pride and joy.

> And they hit me at different periods of time and I can literally re-late certain characteristics I have to specific sisters. [One of them taught me that] you don't quit, you don't give up. You may have started something at the wrong time and you can't com-plete it right now, but it needs to be done and you will do it.

Given this background, it is not surprising that throughout her adult life, Maria's identity has been one of leadership characterized by persistent effort to improve social conditions. For more than thirty years she has been actively involved in various aspects of social ser-vices, from providing direct services to women and children to sitting on the board of various private nonprofit foundations.

Family background can also exert a powerful negative influence. Some of the women's biological family members illustrated what not to do and who not to be. One of three children, Kate experienced her parents' divorce when she was very young. She remembers her fa-ther's side of the family as drinking too much and getting into big fights at family events. "So when my mother actually divorced my fa-ther because he was such a jerk, that was really kind of a happy day in my life." However, that left her mother as the sole support of the fam-ily. "[My father] never paid a dime of child support. Went to great lengths not to do that and it pitched us into a real poverty situation."

Now, at age sixty-one, Kate has reconciled with her father, who is in a nursing home.

> I go down and see him as often as I can . . . and I have accepted the fact that this is my father and the negative things that he im-posed upon me as a child helped mold the person that I am to-day. And for that I'm grateful. Because I look at this man and I say to [my partner], if I ever start acting like my father, slap me hard. I don't want to be like that. He's made me so aware of the kind of human being that I want to be.

TURNING POINTS

A number of the women cited turning points in their lives—the intervention of a mentor, retirement, spiritual experiences, involvement in a political movement, or physical illness—that helped shape their identities. They reflected on specific events that influenced the directions they took in life, the kind of people they became, and how they lived their lives.

Of the women who mentioned turning points, many connected them to their lesbian identity. For example, some women described how they became clearer or more public about their lesbianism after they retired, faced a life-threatening illness, or had a profound spiritual experience. Others related the turning points in their lives to broader identity issues. Some recalled times when they found a place, such as a career, where they felt they belonged. Others described how the women's movement or antigay political initiatives were critical in shaping their lives.

When her parents divorced when she was very young, Greta, now fifty-eight, bounced back and forth between her mother and father. Her early years were not easy. Her mother was "high-strung" and sometimes physically abusive. She recalls a sense of not fitting into her family; she felt isolated even as a very young child.

> I haven't really identified with a family as such even when I was a little kid. Sometimes I would sit and listen and think who are these people anyway? You know, why am I here? Just looking for a place to belong and I knew it wasn't there. . . . I knew that I was different when I started kindergarten. I refused to accept the role that they kept giving little girls and I totally rebelled as early as kindergarten. . . . It was during the war and the boys were soldiers and the girls were nurses and I refused that job. And I had to fight literally to prove that I was capable of being a soldier. And that didn't go over well, but I knew as early as then I was somehow different.

Her sense of alienation and her rebellion continued throughout her early and middle school years. By the time she went to high school she was hanging out with a group of troubled kids, most of whom eventually ended up in jail or worse. However, Greta's teachers intervened and her life took a different direction.

I was signed up for the classes that my friends were in, which was bonehead everything, and these three teachers just went in and took my schedule and changed it and I came back as a sophomore and no amount of anything could get my schedule changed from college prep classes. I was in algebra, I was in biology, language—I couldn't believe my schedule. But no one would listen to me.

None of her family had graduated from high school and although she had been saving money to go to college, Greta credits the intervention and support of these mentors with getting her on track. Now she looks back on her identity as an educator with satisfaction.

I'm very comfortable with the job that I've done in my years in education. I feel good about it. I stay in contact with my students and as I watch— particularly the ones that had the most difficulty—move into really responsible places, it's very rewarding.

Like Greta, Kate wanted to continue her education. Not having the financial means to do so, she joined the military so she could go to college to fulfill her dream of being a history teacher. Just a few months before she was scheduled to get out of the service, she went back home to visit her mother, who had become a nurse. Going to her mother's workplace—the first time she had ever been in a hospital— was a turning point for her. The hospital staff was very welcoming and she ended up staying the whole day.

For the first time in my life I actually felt like I belonged. . . . And I called my mother two days later and I said, "Mom, start looking for a nursing school for me because I want to be a nurse". . . . And from the very first time I ever had direct contact with a patient it has been the most natural feeling in the world. . . . I was almost twenty-one years old before I ever walked into a hospital. And it was just like, this is where I belong. And that's the way it's always been—been doing it now for almost thirty-seven years.

As was mentioned in the previous chapter, retiring allowed a number of the women to publicly identify as lesbian. Having remained closeted for fear of negative reactions, including possibly losing their jobs, they were now free to be more fully themselves. Other turning points resulted in greater self-acceptance as well.

Betty, in her mid-sixties, recalled that when she was thirty she agreed to marry the man she was dating because she was getting older and she felt that's what she was supposed to do. She didn't plan on giving up women and was very upset by the prospect of marriage. She prayed a lot and asked for help from her Higher Power. She described an incident that occurred one night while she was lying in bed.

> All of a sudden there was a big white light in the room. I didn't open my eyes to see it; it's just that it was there. And all of a sudden I thought, I have all the power that I need. All the power! And I thought well, how will I know I have this power? And I just felt, I can remember anything. And I remembered all the phone numbers of all my friends that I'd had when I was a kid, my grandmother's number, our number, and all these phone numbers. Now at this point I was about thirty years old and I was—I hadn't been able to sleep very much for weeks and weeks and weeks. I was so worried about this thing. Then the next morning I thought, well, was that a dream? But I could remember the phone numbers. So it gave me the courage then to give him his ring back and say I couldn't marry him.

Edith's turning point, at age fifty-five, was more physical than spiritual. Now seventy-one, she recounted how she came to identify herself as a lesbian when she reconnected with a friend with whom she had a lesbian experience in college. "I kept in touch with her for many years and went back where she lived . . . and we picked up where we left off thirty years ago." Edith didn't want to come home but had to because she was still married. After a few months of counseling, she got clear about her direction and moved out.

> I have likened it to the fitting of cogs in a template of some sort, where they fit all right in the original position, but that shift— even though it seemed a pretty small shift at the time—just made it fit properly. There are a lot of things about me that didn't change, you know? But certainly my perspective changed.

Political movements also marked turning points for some women. For example, the women's movement has been an important part of life for Beth, age fifty-five.

> Probably the most important thing in my development as a person is the women's movement, getting involved with that in my late twenties—I've stayed involved pretty much ever since then. And certainly that was probably why I went to law school—the sense of social injustice . . . it was a major involvement. I was involved in staffing, I was involved in setting up a feminist women's health center, I was involved in menstrual extraction before *Roe v. Wade*. Stayed involved. Today, I'm treasurer of [a women's political organization].

Many of the women interviewed had experienced health problems—acute as well as chronic. However, most of them described their health as "good," and they tended to see their health issues, and even their disabilities, as something that happened to them rather than something they "were." They often referred to medical issues as a "turning point" or "wake-up call," as a part of the aging process or just as "what was" rather than as a defining part of their identities.

Cancer, in particular, was a major turning point for a number of the women. They described how surviving cancer taught them to try to find something good in every day or to focus on living one day at a time. Audrey, age sixty-three, explained that getting a cancer diagnosis was one of the most difficult times in her life.

> Yeah, it's a real wake-up call. And my partner has been marvelous. She's stood with me through a year that I don't even remember. I was so zonked out on chemo and just sort of lost a year. She was there every inch of the way for me. And I'm fine. I hope. You never know. You keep going from one blood test to the next, but I'm three years out now.

Her experience with cancer changed her attitude about other people's reactions to her being a lesbian.

> I used to worry a lot about that and now I don't. Maybe because I've seen death. You know—this is it. It's a jolt and after that, whether or not somebody's going to disapprove of you because

you're a "homosexual" really doesn't matter a rip. Get your priorities straight.

FINDING MEANING IN LIFE

It is clear that the topic of identity is broad as well as deep. These women's sense of themselves and who they were developed in the context of family and societal influences and included self-definitions based on interpersonal relationships as well as life experiences. A question that served to deepen the inquiry into this topic of identity related to where they found meaning in life. These lesbian elders shared wide-ranging responses to this question. They frequently mentioned relationships with friends, partners, and family members including grandchildren. Activities, the arts, life accomplishments, and spirituality also ranked high on the list.

Laura, age fifty-seven, describes herself as a very spiritual, but not religious, person. She credits her spirituality with providing her the strength to deal with a number of extremely adverse personal situations, including a violent former husband. Although she has given the question of finding meaning in life much thought, she acknowledged that she still was not sure about it.

> I don't know. I have muddled over that question a lot in my life—I don't know what I want to do when I grow up, and I don't really have an answer for that. We think of people, money, prestige, success—I don't really know what gives meaning. I get goodness every day out of something that adds meaning to my life. I do question—I do question sometimes why I am here. And what I am supposed to be doing here while I am here and maybe if I could fully answer that question, then maybe I would know what meaning I could get out of my life. And I don't know. I do believe, like I said before, that I'm on a path, but I don't know why. I don't know where it's leading. I just kind of stay on it because I think I'm supposed to. But that is a question I've wrestled with most of my life. I don't have an answer.

Most of the women responded to the question by identifying specific aspects of their lives that gave meaning. Like Laura, Nell, age sixty-one, survived some very difficult times. After a relationship ended badly, she began a downward spiral that lasted for over four years. During that time she left a successful business, went across the country and back again, floundered in relationships, and filed sexual abuse charges against a former therapist. What gives meaning to her life now is the accomplishment of having survived it.

> I'm mentally a lot stronger and much more—I feel like much more centered and solid. And I don't go way off. I think before I used to just—I was never in the middle. I was way over here or way over there. I'm artistic, I'm creative, and it works really bad when you think of all this crazy stuff you do. A lot of craziness. So I feel like I've accomplished a lot of mental stability, emotional stability.

Stephanie, age fifty-seven, and Janet, age fifty-eight, both identified their connections with people as a meaningful part of their lives. Janet works in a supermarket and described the pleasure of simple everyday interactions with the customers in her workplace.

> I like to make people happy, that means a lot to me . . . especially elderly people, you know? They need that sort of thing. . . . I'm in the back but we're open and I do the case and somebody needs something. I go all the way out on the floor even though I'm in [another] department. And they love it. Yeah, I think for me a lot of meaning in my life is giving—making somebody happy or smile, even if it's just for the moment.

Stephanie used to practice law and then became interested in doing healing practices with women. She finds meaning in intense personal connections.

> I get a real—I get juiced up, usually on one-to-one stuff. Whether I'm working with a client, whether I meet somebody who's relatively new and we spend a couple of hours just really exploring who each other are. I think finding out more about who I am and why I operate and what I can do to put some of the harder parts at ease and put them to rest. It's been fascinating . . . I think part of this is spiritual. I left the church when I was in college and have just considered myself atheist for many, many years, and probably in the last ten years kind of devised my own belief sys-

tem about the universe and how I fit in. That's been really important to giving me a sense of who I am.

Many women mentioned partner relationships as an aspect of their lives where they find meaning. After many years of being alone because she didn't think she could handle intimacy, Nancy, age sixty-two, is involved in a long-term relationship where, "I guess for the first time I feel like I have somebody that truly loves me. For me." During the years she was alone, she helped raise her sister's children, which gave meaning to her life. She also recalled her work being important. "I guess my job was what gave meaning to my life. I was very devoted to my job. Worked a lot of overtime. . . . And now I guess my partner really is what gives meaning to my life."

Denise, age fifty-seven, has been with her partner for twenty-four years.

> I think as a young person I was quite ambitious. I think when you see how fast life goes, your ambitions are tempered with reality and I think one of my biggest ambitions was to be happy with another person, to have a happy life with another person, and I've achieved that.

Because of her partner's disability, they can no longer do some of the things, such as camping, that they used to do. She identified what gives life meaning now.

> Music, books, we both love nature—we've got a bird feeder out here and we watch the birds all the time. . . . I tell you, I just love our little simple daily lives; that is really where I get my nourishment. So that's really it. It's just all the little things that make up a day.

Being active and involved in volunteer work, community service, or political action was very important to a number of the women. Now ninety-five, Madelyn reflected, "The thing that gives meaning to my life is always to be involved and to have some reason to live. Be working on something like what I'm working on now—the right to die."

Helen and her partner met in the military and lived on the West Coast for many years. Her partner died just a few months short of their fiftieth anniversary. Helen, now seventy-three, went into a depression for a few months but then recovered and involved herself in the local gay/lesbian community. Currently she leads discussions at the multiage lesbian support group, and hosts lesbian video nights at her home.

> In spite of the fact that I've had cancer three times . . . I'm in fairly good health and I don't anticipate the aches and pains that most people my age get because I don't allow myself to become stagnant, mentally or physically. . . . As long as the good Lord gives me the energy to keep going, I'll keep volunteering.

Maria, age sixty-three, has a long and extensive history of involvement with community services. What gives meaning to her life is "doing things."

> The world is not perfect and while I believe that our form of government is probably the best in the world, it's lousy. It's a mess. As a result, people constantly get lost through no fault of their own. People are not poor because they want to be poor. They're not uneducated because they don't want to be educated. And those of us who know how to work the system, which is what I'm doing, I learned, it's incumbent upon us to reach back and help, and that's what it's all about. And if you're sitting on your rear end doing nothing, then you're really not part of society as far as I'm concerned. You're outside of it.

Retired from her life work of being a family therapist, Margery, age seventy, spends four mornings a week as the adopted grandmother in a first-grade class. "It fills up my morning time and I feel youthful—youthful, that's interesting. Useful is what I meant to say!" For now, her work with the first graders gives meaning to her life. But she is less clear about the future.

> I could drop dead today and feel that I had accomplished what I wanted to or needed to, so in some ways I kind of dread the next twenty years. I don't have a goal or anything I feel I want to do. I would like to be writing, but I don't know what to be writing about.

Many of the women mentioned gardening, being out in nature, and travel as activities they enjoy and look forward to doing more of. For Pat, age sixty-nine, travel is a lifeline. Since her long-term partner died seven years ago, she has felt very single. "I just try to enjoy every day, make some plan. I find that if I have a travel plan, I am much happier. And you're never lonely on a trip." She travels with Elderhostel because it is an economical way to combine learning with seeing the world and because the other people—even though they are almost always straight—are interesting people who share her passion for art and history.

By far, the most responses to the question about meaning in life were related to spirituality. The beliefs, traditions, and spiritual practices varied widely, but many of the themes were similar. Concepts such as life as a learning process or a journey, the importance of being true to oneself, and the twelve-step principle, "Let go and let God," featured prominently.

For Judy, age fifty-seven, the most dreadful period of her life was being an alcoholic. However, as she pointed out, many very interesting things happened to her as a result. For example, she met a man who became one of her dearest friends while she was at an alcohol treatment clinic. A near-death experience related to her alcoholism also shaped her perspective that life itself is meaningful.

> I don't know whether my life has to have any particular meaning other than being here. . . . People talk about having spiritual experiences and those kinds of things in AA and I never did. Except that on one occasion I found myself—I had been taken to a hospital and I sat up and said to myself, "You know, I really am not supposed to be alive. At this point I really am supposed to be dead. There must be some reason why I am still alive." And I decided at that time, and it was a very intense experience, and I decided that the reason was that I was simply intended to be a part of the ongoing forces of life as opposed to death. That it was not that I was supposed to do great things, solve important problems, or be a great leader or a great intellectual or anything else. I was simply supposed to be part of the ongoing forces of life.

The idea that things are the way they were meant to be, that the individual is the way she is supposed to be and on the path she was meant to be on, was a powerful and recurring theme—expressed in many different ways. At sixty-two, Nancy wishes that she had gone to college, but other than that looks back on her life with no regrets.

> I believe that everything that happens to you is meant to be. Exactly how it happens to you. It's part of what the master plan is for your life. And I don't think you can change anything that's supposed to happen to you. If you're supposed to die today, you'll die today. You're supposed to win the Lotto today, you'll win the Lotto today. . . . I think that even the bad things that happened in my life, that I thought were just devastating at the time, I know there's a reason for that and I guess I've always been willing to accept those things.

Jane has been a Zen Buddhist for the past eleven years. At the time of the interview, she was dying of advanced cancer at age fifty-nine. For her, the question of meaning in life was intertwined with her impending death.

> I just feel that my purpose in life . . .it's to be the very best that I can be . . .and of course that's, in my frame of reference, having integrity . . . just to be a good Zen person, you know, just letting life happen. And I've been a control freak all my life . . . and the one thing I'm learning and getting banged on the head every day about is that I have no control over this. I didn't want to have cancer. I don't want to know that I could die any minute. This isn't something that I would have seen for myself. That's why I saved so I could retire and do stuff like that. And that's not going to happen. That's the way it is. I've been dealt this hand and I just want to do it with dignity.

Ernestine has been a student of Christian Science for over fifty years. Now seventy-five, her identity and sense of meaning come from what she describes as her desire to "grow in grace."

> I wake up and I look for the unfolding of the new day and what the day means to my life and those whom my life touches. And every day I encounter more opportunities to share who I am without imposing upon them or infringing on their space. But I try to make every contact I have worthwhile and to assure the person that they can come to me for help if they need it. If I can be a friend, I'll be there.

Chapter 3

Family

My mother and I were sitting down on the shore. . . . She said. "Eileen, when are you going to get married?" And I said, "Never! I love women." "Good, now we can talk," she said. "Aren't the waves beautiful today?" That was the end of it.

Eileen, age sixty-eight

Of the relationships built throughout life, the most important are those that most would call "family." The concept of family has never been static. Over the centuries it has changed as a result of social and economic shifts such as improved nutrition, political change, industrial revolutions, shifting patterns of migration, and lowered infant mortality due to improved living conditions and medical advances. Its evolution has been cyclical rather than linear, changing as social control alternates with social tolerance. For many of the lesbians interviewed, to be found out by their parents, with great risk of rejection, was an ever-present fear. That fear was exacerbated by the social and political conservatism of the times—from the moral reformers of the 1930s through the McCarthy witch-hunts of the 1950s. During these decades, it was not unusual for parents simply to deny that their daughter was a lesbian or in some cases to disown her. This disowning and denial, for all intents and purposes, denied many lesbians their rightful place in their families of origin.

By most social definitions, only those who are legally or biologically related are considered "family." Although this may reflect the norms of society, in practice there has been a broader definition. Almost everyone can recall a person—a friend, neighbor, "aunt" or "cousin"—who was treated as kin and offered support and resources regardless of biological or legal ties. Although the term "chosen family" was not in use during the early decades of the 1900s, and only used infrequently through the 1960s, many lesbians of that time did, indeed, find their "families" in what today are called chosen families—families composed of partners and close friends as well as children and other biological relatives.

In this chapter we explore the meaning and experience of family among older lesbians. Typically these women described their families as evolving configurations of biological connections and "chosen" family members. The themes of silence and invisibility frequently appeared in their stories about biological family relationships—even when they and their partners were included in family events. Many credited their biological families with important contributions to their development although their relationships with parents and siblings ranged from estranged to strained to very close. Not surprisingly, their experiences among "chosen" family were most often characterized as warm, supportive, and accepting. Relationships with partners and with children were of special significance.

DEFINING FAMILY

The women who were interviewed were asked what the term "family" means to them and whom they include in their families. The meaning of the term "family" differed depending on the situation and experience of each participant. For three-quarters of the women, the definition had changed over time. Early in life they had used the term synonymously with biological family. Later their definitions expanded to include their partners, children, parents, aunts, uncles, cousins, friends, and their community—whether that community was composed of other lesbians, neighbors, or fellow group members.

Amy, age sixty-two, came out in the mid-1950s when she was nineteen. She described herself as "a little bit idiosyncratic," but was never closeted. She was active in lesbian and gay civil rights issues when it was unpopular to be so. Her family never ostracized her because of her lesbianism or her activism. Consequently, she developed a very close family connection. Her immediate family includes herself, her partner, and her partner's children. Her extended family includes many others.

> Well, certainly there's one's biological family, but if we left ourselves stuck with that for a definition, we'd be in a hell of a lot of

trouble, wouldn't we? Now look at my immediate nuclear family. There is a woman [her partner] and two children. Now, certainly that is my definite nuclear family—my partner and these two children. And yes, I have a very extended family biologically. . . . I have nine first cousins and we were pretty much raised together. . . . And we did a lot of family stuff together. . . . [We] are there for each other and we always have been and . . . they are also there for my lover and her children. . . . [T]hen to extend that further, we have close friends who don't have biological family and they are definitely part of our family. . . . And there still exist those lesbians whose families have kicked their butts out, and they have no family even though they might live two blocks away! Well, we need to incorporate those into our families. We have people on Thanksgiving and on Christmas that are part of our family that are not biologically related to us.

Ann, age seventy-one, described the acceptance she received from her parents and her brother as important parts of who she is today. Her parents, with whom she remained close until they died, gave her, her partners, and her friends many positive experiences. Her definition of "family" extended far beyond parents and siblings.

There's family in the sense of my blood relations and I still have close contact with my aunt, who's my mother's only remaining sister who's alive, and my uncle, who's my mother's brother, and my other uncle, and my brother, and my cousin; I have one cousin—that's my family. I guess that the number-one family to me, though, is really the two of us. I mean, we are a couple, and a family doesn't have to be huge. It can be two people. Two people, I think, can make an extremely strong family unit. And then there's the family of our friends. We have these two friends who are straight, and we're all four close and we're good friends. I know that one of them, even though she has a sister, has referred to us as her family. . . . She considers this foursome is really her little family unit here, and she knows that we are lesbians and all; they both do. And then there's the kind of the larger group of friends . . . a whole family of friends.

Many of the women spoke of the idea of family as being an evolving process. Margery, seventy years of age, did not come out until she was in her fifties. She had previously married, had children, and got divorced after eighteen years of marriage. She had internalized her parents' as well as society's homophobia, and had a hard time telling others that she was a lesbian. Several years after she divorced she began dating women. Her concept of family developed and changed as a result of her various relationships. It continues to do so.

> Well, I suppose that's changed over the years because initially it was husband, wife, and children. And now I would say it's any group of people, two or more, who—I was going to say live together. Well, that's one sort of family, and I think there are larger families. I feel very connected to the lesbian community here. I guess I would call that family. I would say that my partner and I are a family. So people of the same sex with children are also families.

Julie is fifty-nine years old and has known she was lesbian since she was in her twenties. She maintains a relationship with her siblings, but she finds her strength and support in her chosen family.

> Well, I have two different families. I have my natural family and I have my chosen family. Generally I like my chosen family better than my natural family. I mean, my natural family— I don't think any of them I would choose to be my friend, my two brothers and my sister and my mother. I mean, it's not that they—it's just they wouldn't be people probably that I would seek out to be friends with. My sister and I used to be good friends, but that's kind of drifted apart. She lives here too, and we still get along fine and everything, but our social circles have sort of drifted apart. But when I think of family, I think about if I were critically ill in the hospital— my family that I would expect to have around are all women friends that we have. [They] are just wonderful and when any member of our group has some kind of a difficult time or anything, everybody's there. They're there and they'll be there.

Although the majority of the women described "family" as having several facets, some defined "family" strictly in terms of biology. Many spoke of how it was during their earlier years when they could not safely be open about their sexual orientations. Several women described how they maneuvered through family settings.

At fifty-seven, Stephanie is one of the younger women who participated in the study. She married in her late thirties and had a child before she realized she was lesbian. Although she was very close to her father, her mother remained more distant. She now has a very close relationship with her daughter, who is also lesbian. Stephanie's definition of "family" is based on kinship.

> I suppose I still, when I hear that, think of biologic family. And when I think of family as it is often used in gay and lesbian contexts, that is the association, voluntary. I think I use the word community for that, I guess.

Despite becoming aware of being lesbian when she was in her twenties, Kay lived a totally closeted life until she retired at age sixty-six. Now seventy-one, she has had many personal and professional accomplishments of which her family is proud, but she has never been able to discuss her partners with her family. This has created a distance between her and her relatives.

> My mother died in childbirth, and I was raised by a maternal aunt and uncle, [my mother's] sister and her husband. They were really my parents, they were quite a bit older than I; they were my family, and the only living relative that I recognize much is my one hundred-year-old aunt who was my biological father's sister. He (my biological father) and his wife were friendly, but usually when I went to their place to visit, I took a man with me. It was a gay man generally, in earlier years, but they didn't know that. . . . They must have known. You know, I didn't marry for so many years. Hell, I haven't been married since 1949; that was my last divorce. You can only be between marriages so far! I've been in between marriages since 1949. So I'm sure that—and I've lived with women most of this time and they've been very accepting but never discussed at all. That was my family. I have a half-brother and a half-sister, two half-brothers and a half-sister; I'm not close to them, never was raised with them. I know them; they're like cousins. When I go to these family reunions, I see all these cousins and people, but I don't feel close to any of them.

One participant, Jane, age fifty-nine, indicated that she had no family, no biological relatives, and no relationships that she considered her family. Terminally ill with cancer, she viewed the concept of family from her position as a dying woman.

> I think one of the hardest experiences about having advanced cancer, meaning that I'm going to die any minute—any minute—for various reasons: I could get a stroke, I could throw a clot, that sort of thing. And I don't have family. I have no blood family. I have a brother in Oregon, and we talk on the phone, and I think one of the most disappointing things for me was the fact that there is no family for me. People are wonderful for the first week or two weeks and then they're gone. I mean they're gone. Periodically people will show up and then they're gone. So I have not experienced any real consistency. My friend that was coming down and spending a couple or three weeks with me, I paid her, that sort of thing. I've been sick now for three years and people come in for a while and then they leave and others come in and then they leave. It's scary. Because there's no support and [it] is such an illusion.

BIOLOGICAL FAMILY

When describing their relationships with their immediate families, many of the women said that once the family discovered that they were lesbians they were no longer welcome in the family, were barely tolerated, or told to get cured. Some said that, over time, their relationships with their parents or siblings had improved, but others never resolved the tension or hostility.

For many of the women, their mothers' reactions were muted or silent. Eileen, age sixty-eight, described how her intended coming out met with her mother's denial.

> Way back when I was real young, back in the 1940s, you just didn't talk about stuff like that. I tried to come out to my folks. One time I was visiting, not too long ago—maybe twenty years ago or something—my mother and I were sitting down on the shore. We lived in Duluth, Minnesota, right on Lake Superior, and she said, "Eileen, when are you ever going to get married?"

And I said, "Never! I love women." "Good, now we can talk," she said. "Aren't the waves beautiful today?" That was the end of it.

Other women never formally came out to their families. They simply lived their lives and let their families think what they would. Joan, at seventy, said her family knew that she was gay but no one ever discussed it with her. Similar to several of the women interviewed, Joan described a certain silence about her sexual orientation, which ultimately led her not to participate in some family functions.

> I think my brother knew, but my mom, you know, I think she knew but she didn't know what she knew. She was really a very nice woman and just a real loving parent unconditionally and so forth. And so the first lady I did live with, I lived with for about eight years and then—the old story—we broke up. And I can remember my mother being quite upset with me about it, quite frankly. So I think she knew but didn't know what she knew, you know? Maybe they don't. They think it's not really the norm, but she didn't really know what being homosexual was, I don't think. She wasn't the kind that read a lot of books. So, my family just sort of accepted it. But I find that I stayed away a lot from family things.

The parents of many of the participants were deceased and never knew about their daughters' sexual orientation. Relationships with siblings and extended family, often being less strained than those with parents, played a significant role in the women's lives.

Laura, at fifty-seven, is a mother and grandmother with a very large extended family. Although she has never formally come out, she spoke of a family setting that encouraged acceptance and independence. Laura described her family relationships from the perspective of family gatherings, a situation where underlying assumptions are made and codes of silence are kept.

> We have been doing a family picnic since—I think 1927. . . . It has never been that one of the members of my family that was gay or lesbian has not brought a significant other. Sometimes it's the same one year to year; sometimes it's not, depending on the relationship. . . . As each generation comes along, there are

gay member[s] of our family through each it, but they introduce their friends to all of us who are known to be gay . . . they will just come up and say, "This is my auntie," . . ."This is my friend Susie," whatever. . . . So, you may come to a family picnic and you may see whatever you see! All nationalities, all sizes, all shapes, all whatever. And . . . when I speak of the family, I'm talking about aunts, uncles, my mother, whatever the oldest generation was there—they never have thrown anyone out of the picnic and they never talk, because we are in every family. So the pot can't call the skillet black, okay?

As with Laura's family, silence did not always equal a lack of knowledge about a gay family member's orientation. Even when it wasn't discussed, the women's families often knew about their lesbianism. And sometimes, great openness led to better understanding. Eileen, at sixty-eight, has always lived openly as a lesbian, even though she did not discuss her sexual orientation with some members of her immediate family. She has two sisters and a large extended family. She described what happened when she came out to her sisters.

Well, the one from California knew evidently all the time, never said anything, so when I came out to her it was just like, "So are you telling me something I don't know?" The other one was scared to death of us and came to visit and found that we were a normal family sort of thing, and she's been fine.

Getting involved in the political activities of the time enabled Eileen to more directly involve family in her efforts to help defeat an antigay initiative.

Now, when they had that Initiative 9 or that thing down in Oregon, trying to get the gays out of there—I've got relatives there. I had relatives who've since died, an aunt and an uncle and some cousins—well, they were going to have this vote and so I wanted to help. In fact I went to a rally downtown and they said, "If you've got any way to help, help." Well, I did. So I wrote to my aunt and I came out to her, and she wrote back and she didn't say, "I always knew it," or "I'm so glad you said something," or "Oh my God. I can't stand this thought." She just said, "I called your uncle and all these cousins and I told them all to vote against this thing."

Elaine is fifty-seven years old and also has lived openly as a lesbian. Although her mother initially had difficulty accepting her coming out, Elaine reported that she is supportive now and frequently asks about Elaine's involvement in gay and lesbian events. Elaine's openness has also led to very close and supportive relationships with her sisters.

> My younger sister lives here and I'm helping her on weekends—she and my brother-in-law are building a home and I'm going down and working with them. My other sister's in the eastern part of the state. And they're able to tease me about my sexual orientation. They're very comfortable, and my sister— my nieces are in their early twenties now; one's married—but many years ago my sister said, "I think when you're ready, you need to explain to [the nieces] what a lesbian is, because I want them to hear the correct story. I want them to hear what it is really, and not all these stupid rumors that go around." So, we're close.

Of the women who have children, almost all mentioned a special sensitivity to the reaction of their children. Believing it was better for the children to keep the family intact, some stayed with their husbands long after they knew they were lesbian. Even those who left their marriages and lived with lesbian partners usually waited until their children were older—often grown and gone—before coming out explicitly to them. Some expressed regret that this secrecy was hard on their children. However, although hiding may have been "no way to live," their fears for themselves and for their children led them to believe there was no alternative. Those who were less secretive had to work through predictable reactions such as jealousy of the new partner, anger at not having been told earlier, and children wondering if they are gay.

Margery, a therapist, is seventy years old and retired from private practice. She is considered an authority on child abuse. She is actively involved in a women's resource and sponsoring organization. Margery said her idea of family was evolving, as was her relationship with her children. One of Margery's children, in particular, had difficulty with the family changes that occurred as a result of his mother's first lesbian relationship.

> When I first got together with my first partner at fifty, my youngest child was fifteen and was still at home, and his brother was nineteen and was at home at the time. And I'd had other female roommates in the house, and it worked out really well. And so she moved in and I don't know where my head was—I knew I was very clear that I would never remarry while I had teenagers, but this was different. I don't know. Anyway, my fifteen-year-old who everyone liked, boys, girls, parents, teachers—he really was and is a charming person—suddenly became sullen and difficult. My partner was much younger than I, and I felt like I was caught between two fifteen-year-olds. And I wanted to sit down with her and talk to him and she wouldn't do it, and I didn't have the guts to do it myself. It was a bad scene. She finally moved out of the house and we continued our relationship and the very next day he was his old self again. And he said at one point, "I don't like her trying to be part of our family. So, what you do outside of this house is okay, but don't get any of it off on me, I guess." Anyway, now he's just fine with it. And my other two children—my nineteen-year-old, it was time for him to move out, and he did move out, and I don't know whether it was because of her or not. It just happened that way. Then that left my youngest to fend for himself, which wasn't easy. And I have since cleared the air with my youngest about that. He was really hurt, thought I had chosen her over him. And that I no longer supported him the way I had in the past. And, in some ways he was right.

Jean, fifty-six years of age, came out in her thirties after having been married and having a child. She grew up in a radical, politically active family, which was difficult for her because of their social prominence. She defined family along lines of the "past" and "present," with the past representing biological family members, and the present including the people she chooses as family. Jean's daughter is an important part of her chosen family. Like many teenagers, her daughter experienced questions about her own sexuality when her mother came out to her. Jean discussed how her daughter's acceptance evolved.

My kid had a hard time in the beginning and she felt like she had to hide it, and now she's really proud of me and she finds, I think, that there's a little bit of attractiveness to having a mother who's lesbian. But she's also talked to me about how it ends up being really confusing to her, about her own sexuality—"What do I do about my best friend? I think I've been in love with her all my life, Mom, but what do I do about it?" I say, "It's up to you."

For many of the women, coming out signaled the end of a long-term marriage. No matter how open and accepting the family, this change was often accompanied by difficulties and a period of adjustment. Sometimes, different children in a family adjusted at different rates. Sharon, now fifty-nine, married and had two children before coming out and establishing a long-term relationship with a woman. She described her children's transition to a new family situation.

When I left to move in with my former partner, the one I was with for twenty years, I left the kids with my ex-husband because I didn't want to jerk them out of schools and stuff. And we got an apartment that was walkable from the house. My daughter was eight and my son was twelve, just turning twelve, I guess. And he wasn't even surprised. He was very accepting. [My daughter] was a little harder to win over. She had a harder time with it, I think. Maybe because she was a woman and she was afraid it was like chickenpox, or something—she might catch it too. And I think she was very protective of her father and she was probably concerned that what I was doing was going to hurt him, and I think it probably did hurt him, but he accepted it. Both of the kids were very accepting.

Children can also be a major source of strength for a parent, and when a parent is lesbian, the support of her children and grandchildren is a special gift. Several of the women saw their relationships with their children as a positive influence. In the 1950s, Ellen knew she was gay but was not comfortable with that due to myriad social pressures. She subsequently married and had three children before coming out in her fifties. For Ellen, age sixty-two, her adult children are a major support for her.

I have a daughter and two sons, and she's the one that I talk to the most, and she said it's just not a factor. "You're my mommy, I love you, I love your partner too, you know, it's okay. It's nothing you have to apologize to me for, or anything, just be yourself." Her daughter, my four-year-old—soon to be five-year-old—granddaughter was coming up to spend the night. Well, whenever she spent the night up here, she always slept with me.... And I talked with my daughter and I said, "Well, I want my granddaughter to sleep on either the floor, the bed, or the living room or what have you, like the boys do when they come up. And so, try to gear her toward that way of thinking. Or we can put a special mattress for her down in [my partner's] office." And when it came time, I asked my daughter if she'd said anything to my granddaughter, and she said, "No, Mom. I don't want to make a big deal out of it because it isn't a big deal. Wherever you want her to be, that's fine." . . . Well, my granddaughter fell asleep here on the floor while we were watching TV, so when she woke up she didn't know where she was. Well, next thing I knew, she's wrapped—she's crawled up into my partner's arms in bed and she was sleeping there, and my partner rolled over and put her between us. And she slept here the rest of the night. Nothing was ever said one way or another, so my daughter says, "That's what I was hoping. I didn't want to do any prompting or anything, because there's nothing wrong." So I thought that was great. So I think I'm following my daughter's example—just don't pay any attention to it, just go ahead and go about our business and see what happens.

THE LESBIAN FAMILY: PARTNERSHIPS AND RELATIONSHIPS

For many women, their long-term partners became their families. All the partnered women defined themselves and their partner as a family, with most identifying their partner as their most important family. Other important family members were children, other relatives, and members of their social groups and the lesbian community. Several of the women are in partnerships that have lasted ten years or longer, with some in partnerships of fifteen, twenty, or more than thirty years. The women described a range of factors key to maintaining a successful long-term partnership, including commitment, communication, trust, love, work, and equality.

Edith is seventy-one years old. Aside from a college romance, she has had two committed relationships: her marriage of twenty-eight years and her current eleven-year partnership. Commitment has always been important to Edith and is a key element in who she is. She defines commitment as "an attitude."

> It's always been, either figuratively or literally speaking, that if I have given my word about something, then that holds. I think part of that is my generation. I think that there were a lot of marriages when I was growing up that probably should have ended, including my parents', had it been a more open climate for divorce. But I think that I certainly grew up with the attitude that you make that kind of a commitment and it is a commitment and you do your best to make it work.

When Ann, also seventy-one, talked about her long-term relationship with her partner, she described a previous relationship that illustrated the importance of communication.

> I guess some of it comes with maturity. I think for one thing, I've learned some things that can be very difficult in a relationship and when my current partner and I got together, we discussed these things. . . . My first love was—it was wonderful and all, but she was moody and she was an actress and she would get, for some reason, she would get into a mood and she would, at that point, the way she reacted was that she cut off communications. So suddenly she wouldn't be talking to me and I wouldn't know what I had done. And I always thought I had done something— see, that's that old guilt thing. . . . It still upset me all the time because I'm a person that wants to communicate. And so I told my current partner, I said, "Communication is very important to me. And if I do something that really ticks you off and you get upset about it, I want you to tell me so I will know and all. Don't shut up and go off somewhere and put your head in a box or something, or don't make me feel that I'm sitting out here on an ice floe somewhere."

Love and trust were intertwined concepts for many of the women. Ann described love as "not a possession. . . . If you really love someone, they're not something you're going to fold up and put in a box and drive nails in the top, and all of that." With such openness often came vulnerability. Jennifer, now sixty, had been in a long-term relationship that ended when her partner met someone new. She described her thoughts about that betrayal: "I think a relationship—when that trust is broken, you can't go back. It's never the same."

Others more successfully navigated the waters of long-term commitment. Helen, at seventy-three, has been partnered for almost fifty years. She described her relationship as

> Forever. Just forever. And I would guess maybe ten years or so into the relationship, when I was still raging hormones and lacking discretion, I was tempted here and there along the line to step outside the relationship, but I never did. Neither did she. Ever.

To make relationships work, many women mentioned that each partner must be committed to working on each part of their lives together. Even those who stated that they and their partners are different in many ways articulated specific areas in which they worked well as couples. Ellen, now sixty-two, experienced a number of short-term relationships with women during the time she served in the military as well as during her marriage and for a while after her divorce. She currently is now in what she calls her first long-term relationship, which just passed its one-year mark. She hopes for many more. On looking back she said that what she learned was that to make a relationship work requires a lot of work.

> I guess when I was young and got married, I thought you got married and that was it, you know. As I've grown more mature and stuff, I realize that the relationship, the beginning, might just be something that happens, but it takes work for two people to keep it going, and I often equate it to the three-legged stool. One is me and one is you and one is our relationship, and all three have got to be standing on their own to keep that stool up. I think it should be worked on and we both are doing that. I keep waiting for an argument, though, to find out if we can survive an

argument: "Please get mad at me about something!" But I realize how special relationships are, and they don't just survive on their own. That might be the only change I have now from then—I thought you put a ring on your finger and that was it. That gave me license to change him and he to change me—and it didn't work. Sometimes it's hard—I do things and she does things another way. I'm the analyst and this kind of stuff, and she's kind of—very different from me. So, we're doing okay. Let me be me and you be you and this sort of stuff, and that has always been hard for me because I'm quite a controller, and I have to keep aware of that. Because I know the way things should be.

Some of the women sought to achieve equality in their lesbian partnerships. Kay's previous partnerships with women were long-term, fun, and good, but a sense of balance seemed to be missing. As she discussed her current relationship, Kay compared the sense of equality she has in her current partnership with that of past relationships.

I feel that for the first time in my life I have a relationship with an equal, and this was something that has always been important to me. I felt very much love with the men I married, both of them, but I was never an equal—society won't allow that. Because they're the Somebody and you're Mrs. Somebody. I didn't like that. Then I was with a woman for eight years, who was an assistant to me. We went to law school together, but she never— it wasn't an equal relationship. Then I lived with another one for twenty-five years who was many years younger than I—fourteen years younger, I think—and she went to college and she got a bachelor's degree, but we didn't really have what I would call an equal relationship. We lived together, we worked together, it was fun, it was a nice comfortable relationship, but it wasn't one of equality. And at this time in my life, for the last eight years, I've been with this woman who also has a PhD, who has as much money as I do, who can support herself, pay her way, whose values are the same as mine, and it's a very comfortable kind of relationship—for the first time in my life. And this is something I have always wanted, to be on an equal basis with a person. I don't want somebody who's taking care of me, and I don't want to take care of somebody. However, as old as we are, if one of us gets sick, I'm sure that will be the case. You would take care of somebody.

Chapter 4

Work

What has really changed my life more than anything inside me is that I've broken barriers of—what do you call it— discrimination.

Ernestine, age seventy-five

Our occupations and the fields in which we work can mean much to the other facets of our lives because they are often linked to our identities and sense of accomplishment—as well as to our survival. The history of what work has been available to women is ever evolving, with the greatest advances having occurred in only the last three or four decades. Before the 1970s, types of jobs were largely separated by gender, with men's positions commanding higher pay and prestige, while women worked at traditionally female jobs with less pay. Furthermore, there was no expectation that women would be working in order to support themselves or their families; their wages were generally viewed to be supplemental to a husband's earnings. Between the 1920s and the 1970s, very few women were in positions of power, either politically or in the corporate sector, who could influence a need for change, and a very real fear of being labeled a lesbian kept most women from trying. In the 1970s, pressure from the feminist movement, civil rights movement, the Equal Employment Opportunity Commission (EEOC), and federal legislation under Title IX removed gender restrictions for work. Yet even with these changes, substantial obstacles to equality at the workplace still impede a woman's ability to acquire various types of work and the pay and status she deserves.

Lesbians have faced additional challenges. Regardless of age or historical context, most lesbians need to support themselves financially and plan for their retirements. At the same time, they have been at great risk of losing their employment because being gay was reason enough for dismissal. Since it was not until 1973 that the American Psychiatric Association removed homosexuality from its list of mental illnesses, firing a lesbian could be justified on the basis of her "sexual perversion." Those working in education and with children felt particularly vulnerable. Almost all workplaces were extremely homophobic and the military was particularly punitive.

As we see in this chapter, the overwhelming majority of elder lesbians interviewed remained closeted on the job or adjusted their career plans or both. Almost all lived with the fear of exposure and the potential loss of livelihood. We also find that self-identified lesbians in the 1930s, 1940s, and 1950s faced a different situation in their career choices and working lives than those women who married and came out later, when the culture and work environments were more accepting.

Despite these difficulties, work provided opportunities and a sense of accomplishment. For some women the primary role of work was to earn money to survive, provide security, and to finance a retirement. Others took pleasure in the work itself or in the opportunities it provided for developing relationships, learning more about themselves, breaking down barriers, and increasing opportunities for other women. Many of the women made their first contact with other lesbians as well as met partners at the workplace. Whether they worked at many different jobs or held the same job for thirty years, or whether they pursued highly paid professional careers or scrambled to make ends meet, working meant independence.

WORK AND SEXUAL IDENTITY

When they discovered their sexual orientation, some women found their early career dreams dashed. As a teenager, Elaine, age fifty-seven, realized that she would be forced to change her plans.

> I also was going to become a youth minister at one point, and it dawned on me in high school that there was no way the church was going to let me work with kids. I wasn't totally out. I was still struggling with my identity, but that was very painful when I realized that probably that avenue would be closed. . . . I knew I could never be a youth minister . . . and that was devastating, and

I thought, well, then I decided—I just turned my back on anything religious. . . . It really forced me into looking at some issues of who I was and where I wanted to be.

Others sought to keep their career goals by tailoring, or even elimi-
nating, their social lives to accommodate the requirements of their careers. To put it more succinctly, many women decided to live a double
life. Maria, a retired teacher who recognized her lesbianism early on,
opted to hide her sexual orientation.

After I finished college and even during college—during my
last year of college—I stopped going to gay bars. I was going to
be a teacher and I was afraid of being picked up. And then I entered the closet, very nicely, very well, very easily. [I] had a lot
of gay male friends and we did everything together.

Even when it required being in the closet, work still provided
women with the chance to meet one another. A variety of jobs, especially factory work, provided a means to discover others—or have
them discover you—as well as a chance to be openly subversive by
wearing pants. Married at sixteen and divorced two years later, Joan
held a number of jobs over her seventy years. She recalls how working in factories brought women together.

I think part of it is that it was during the Second World War. . . .
There were a lot of women working in plants, war plants. . . .
I went to work at a . . . [military] supply depot at that time. And
of course I met other women that I was attracted to and I
couldn't quite understand and, of course, someone has to drag
you out. So I ran into several friends there. But prior to that I
worked at [a factory]. . . . I remember this Rosie the Riveter. And
I was in transportation and she was working on this airplane
over there, and I was just really fascinated by her without really
knowing why. . . . [Then] I met these other lesbian women and
finally realized the situation. . . . [W]ell, once somebody picks
you out and you're having an affair or whatever, then the book's
open. Then they tell you what's out there, that there are other
women and it's not wrong to care about other women, that
you're not nuts, that you're not the only one in the world. But
someone has to tell somebody that's just the way it goes. . . . It

was a little bit harder. But once you make that connection—and of course during the war it brought a lot of women out to the workforce.

LESBIANS IN THE MILITARY

Historically, joining the military represented an opportunity for women to work, live independently, and not rely on family or marriage for financial support. During the Civil War, women—disguised as men—served in the ranks, from doctors to privates. Others served in more gender-acceptable positions, such as nurses and cooks, while still others filled the ranks of camp followers. World War I saw women ambulance drivers, nurses, and limited women's auxiliary units. World War II opened the doors further. Large numbers of women—lesbian and straight—joined out of patriotism, to leave home, and the chance to expand their opportunities. Some women joined organizations such as the Civil Air Patrol or went to work in war plants. Although the demands of war did allow women to move beyond the accepted role of homemaker, it did not really lead to lasting change. At the end of war the military led the push to get women back into the home and traditional roles.

Those who pursued careers in the military met with rigidly enforced heterosexuality. Civilian life, in spite of its intolerance of differences, allowed at least a semblance of a choice regarding being out or closeted—and to what degree. The military did not. For the most part, the military kept its forces free of homosexuals after World War II by driving them underground through fear generated by witch-hunts and court-martials based on less than legal evidence.

The hypocrisy of these policies is, and was, more than obvious. Many of those enforcing antihomosexual regulations were themselves gay or lesbian and were recognized as such by those they were required to bring charges against—a situation that often became unbearable and destructive. Rhonda, now sixty, spent twenty-one years in the military. She'd had a successful career and at the time was one of the highest-ranking women officers. However, institutionalized homophobia and hypocrisy made it impossible for her to continue her career.

Could have been longer but I got out as a [commanding officer]. And I would say the driving factor was being a lesbian. . . . I did not have to [leave]; I got out early just going up for [promotion]. . . . It was a question of integrity. How much longer was I going to put up with having to lie and be in the closet? Even then, in 1980, we had a "don't ask, don't tell"—that understanding. If I don't tell, they won't ask. And if I were discovered, it's up and out. [It] very definitely took a toll on my inner self and integrity. Here I'm supposed to be an upstanding, outstanding . . . officer, and yet I'm violating a rule, a major rule. I think the crowning blow was when I had, as a CO, to discharge about six people at different times for homosexuality. How does that feel? I just couldn't live that way anymore, could not deny who I am.

In many ways, Rhonda's experience in the military continued in her civilian life: The stigma of lesbianism did not go away and she still struggled with being fully out. Adding to these problems was a gnawing resentment of feeling pressured to leave the military.

I wanted [it to be okay] to stay in . . . as a lesbian who doesn't flaunt her lesbianism but is comfortable enough, and to lift this "don't ask, don't tell." And to have made [CO], and maybe [top rank], that's where I was headed. I didn't finish my career. I still have dreams about the [military] and about not finishing. It was my choice, but it really wasn't my choice.

Anxiety, fear, and resentment of the arbitrary use of hypocritical policies regarding homosexuals were not limited to officers such as Rhonda. It was democratically shared with the lower ranks. All were, on the one hand, shoved vigorously into the closet and, on the other hand, yanked out of it to experience inquisitions or court-martials, or both. Many of the women who had been in the military described the witch-hunts they were subjected to, particularly during the 1950s and 1960s, in order to purge the military of gays and lesbians.

Although some officers, such as Rhonda, were terribly disturbed by the role they were required to play in "catching" lesbians, others simply took the position that self-preservation came first. While she was serving in the [military], Nancy, sixty-two years old, found herself caught between a homophobic [officer] who wanted her court-martialed and a [officer] whom everyone knew was gay, but who would not substantiate Nancy's statement that she was not present when an alleged lesbian act took place. Nancy was discharged.

> Eventually we were all kicked out of the [military]. They started their investigation and it was horrible. It was really the most horrible thing I've ever gone through. Well, they call you to OSI, their Office of Special Investigation, and they call you off your job and first they offer you a cigarette if you're a smoker. And I found out later that it was because they want to see how you held it. If you hold a cigarette down here, on your fingers, that's the way a man holds a cigarette. That's the thing they went by—all the stereotypes. Well, some of us did and some of us didn't. Most of us, I guess, held our cigarette like a man. That's what they wanted to see. And then they'd put you in a room and let you sit there for a half-hour or so by yourself with nothing to do. And then they'd come in and say, well, so and so's already said that they were lesbians, so you might as well tell us what you know about them. And they'd lie. Mostly they'd lie. And they have no conscience, and at that time they were all men—didn't give a damn about anything except what they could drag out of you. They followed us around when we took three-day passes or went home for weekends. They knew everything we did, every place we went. There was probably, I'd say, at least a dozen of us involved in this. And of course their main objective was to get rid of us as a group. . . . The [officer] was gay as well, and we knew that she was but she wouldn't dare stand up for any of us. So I was discharged after a little over a year in the service—the [officer] told me I'd be the first to go and I was.

Eligibility for investigation could be anything from being reported by an anonymous source to associating with a suspected or known homosexual, as Evelyn discovered. Of Midwestern background, raised a Catholic and just out of high school, she joined the military when she was eighteen. Her previously circumscribed knowledge of lesbians was remedied by being in the military. She left the military after serving her enlistment, obtained a journalism degree, and joined the staff of a West Coast paper. Now fifty-five, she is still a journalist.

> I was walking through and these new [recruits] checked in at the base and they were from my hometown. . . . [Joyce] went to

the rival Catholic school—I went to Immaculate Conception, she went to St. Joseph's, we didn't know one another but there we were. . . . I thought she was cute . . . but I didn't pay a lot of attention, and so we were on the ball team together and it just happened that I was catcher, and she was pitcher. . . . And I was in her room one day and the first baseman was her roommate—she was totally gay. I never heard the word "gay" until I went in the service, you know, from a Catholic background. And all I knew was that it was something you're supposed to stay away from. . . . [I]n the [military] at that time it was very difficult. . . . In the [service] if you're associated with anyone who is found to be gay, you're considered gay. Pow, that was that. And actually our whole ball team was put under scrutiny. We actually had quite a mixture of gay and straight, but the pitcher and the first baseman were going together. They went home one year, then they were picked up later and that was rather awful. They put you under armed guard and marched you back and forth to the chow hall. It was dehumanizing, humiliating, and embarrassing—it was awful. I was called in because of them—they threatened me with court-martial . . . and I was scared. I mean, I was still a kid and they told me they would notify my parents and they would have to come into court. But I took a lie detector test and passed it. Because the questions they asked me were not what was happening. They just picked the wrong questions.

Denise was not as fortunate. The fear tactics used during her investigation and the stigma of being discharged had lasting consequences. Now enjoying the best time in her life at age fifty-seven, Denise recalled being kicked out of the military, the struggles that resulted, and the fear afterward as probably the hardest time in her life.

One day I was suddenly whisked off to the Central Intelligence Agency [sic] in New York City . . . where I was really, really drilled for a long time, with our [service] officer present. And my partner was brought in and we weren't allowed to speak to each other, only to our attorney. . . . [I received an] undesirable discharge and I went to Washington, DC, to work. And that was hard because I was so worried about getting a job. They told me that I would be, you know, I could never be bonded. They really scared the bejesus out of you. Oh gosh, Washington, DC, was just full of all these gay women who'd been in the [military] and who'd gotten out one way or another. . . . They had all kinds of horror stories to tell. One gal, every time they told her that they were going to bond her, she just never went back to work again. She just went and got another job. Well, I just was terrified about it because of the tales I had heard, but I went ahead and I was scared to death all the time that someone was going to find out that I'd been in the [military], because I had to cover those two years. I couldn't say I'd been in the [military]. I never had a problem except that fear really shapes your life. I mean I lived with that fear a lot and it was very hard on me for a long time.

Civilians working for the military were not exempt from scrutiny and experienced much the same witch-hunts and oppression as did military personnel. Even volunteer work required a double life. Shirley, now eighty-one, was a volunteer with the Civil Air Patrol during World War II. Later on when she discovered that she was a lesbian, she also discovered that she could not talk about it. It was made very clear that talking about such things had definite consequences.

They explained that they had to be very, very careful or they'd be drummed out of the corps. And I said, "Why is that?" And they said, "We could be blackmailed." And I said, "If everybody knew, there'd be no reason for blackmail. What the hell is the reason then?" And they said, "Well, that's the way it is." And [that made me very angry]. They said, "You could be thrown out of the Civil Air Patrol." And I said, "For Christ's sake, it's voluntary! I go out and risk my fool neck. Nobody pays me. I pay my own way, and they can throw me out?" . . . So then I became aware of what was—you know, the way it is.

Even then, Shirley "never made any great effort to conceal [her] lifestyle." She may not have talked about being lesbian, but she did not make any effort to hide it. She was then—and still is—very much ahead of her time in claiming her identity.

WORK AND THE DOUBLE LIFE

The military may have epitomized—and even institutionalized—a homophobic work environment. However, most of the women viewed their job as a primary reason to be in the closet whether they were in the military or not. What was important was their experience with a continuing negative public awareness of lesbianism and the related public policy designed to force women out of professions deemed un-womanly—such as college professors, law, and medicine—into mar-riage and "acceptable," womanly jobs. Teaching, at any level, was one of many professions that required living a double life or facing the prospect of being discharged.

Frances, age fifty-five, taught school for many years before chang-ing careers to work with developmentally disabled people. Through-out her teaching career, she lived in fear that she would be found out and took measures to prevent discovery.

> I hid it for many, many years because I didn't want anybody to know. I was afraid for my job. Probably would have been fired especially when I became a schoolteacher. I taught for several years—fifteen to twenty. . . . I felt I would be laid off, or in some way dismissed, you know. . . . I'm at the point now where I'm not, guess the term is "closeted," anymore although I don't come out openly and say that I'm gay. . . . I used to date [a gay man]. We used to go out together and faked it. . . . That was part of the facade when I felt I had to do that.

Frances's fear was well founded. State laws made it extremely easy to have homosexual teachers fired. Another teacher, Audrey, now in her early sixties, had married, had two children, divorced, and raised the children. All during this time it troubled her deeply that she could not be honest about who she was, since she was a teacher in the Pacific Northwest.

Such fear of exposure and its consequences permeated all occupa-tions—from youth organizations such as the Girl Scouts to the tele-phone company. For Val, age fifty-seven, her situation as a journalist differed little from that of many teachers.

> And then, of course, in the newspaper business, I had to be very careful . . . particularly at the paper I retired from . . . because my lover was on the paper and we had a homophobic publisher. . . . I had to be, for financial—well, for survival.

Ruth, age fifty-eight, who was neither a teacher nor a journalist, did experience the direct consequences of exposure. When not at her office job, she spent every minute she could with small theater groups. When Ruth asked her supervisor for time off "because I was rehearsing a show with the drag queens downtown," she lost her position.

> Well word got around, whisper, whisper in the office. I didn't know what to do. They were . . . planting very important documents in my wastebasket . . . and other things to make me look bad. Oh, then they were going to offer me another job. . . . I knew nothing about and I knew I would fail the first day because the job announcement said the person had to have training in this particular skill. So the following Friday they just said pack up your stuff, we'll walk you to your car. That was it.

Even having her own business did not necessarily save a woman from living a double life. Although Kay is now seventy-one years old and "very much out of the closet," she "stayed in the closet in order to make a living." As a mental health care worker and expert witness, Kay feared the loss of her "successful practice with a lot of people who were somewhat homophobic" and the loss of income if it became known that she was a lesbian. She also believed that being out would negatively affect her position within the court system.

WORK SATISFACTION

Despite the homophobia of many workplaces and the stresses of leading a double life, work was a source of great pride and satisfaction for many of the women. They took pride in making their own way in the world, in doing a good job, in demonstrating that women could do the work that previously had been done only by men, in making positive changes in the lives of others, and in giving back to the community. Some wanted work to be fun, others thrived on facing difficult challenges and overcoming obstacles. Whether the work was blue, pink, or white collar, the sense of accomplishment made work a positive experience for some, while for others the interpersonal contacts and relationships they developed provided satisfaction.

Christine, age sixty-four, has been driving a bus in her small community for thirteen years. Over the years, she has grown to know her riders to the point that she has come out to some of them. She described herself as a recovering alcoholic, and a Catholic, who for years was wracked with guilt for being a lesbian, to say nothing of feelings of inadequacy as a parent, which for the most part she has overcome. She is hoping to complete a book soon focusing on bus drivers and their riders.

> [Driving a bus] has never been just a job. It's an exchange of ideas; it's a camaraderie that develops . . . between [riders and their bus drivers]. And I like my riders; I like working with people. It can be just a really dumb, grungy kind of job, but it isn't most of the time for me. . . . I take pride in my work.

Ernestine, now seventy-five, has worked at many different jobs and enjoyed almost all of them. She described herself as having always been ambitious and able to provide for herself, even at a very young age.

> What has really changed my life more than anything inside me is that I've broken barriers of—what do you call it—discrimination. In World War II, I left a bank job and went to work as a welder and worked until the war was over. And there were only twenty women in the whole shipyard with like 5,000 men. There were seven welders and thirteen burners, and I was a big 108 pounds, barely five foot three. Since I was so small, they gave me all those jobs that needed to be in the bosun's chair up on the mast or underneath the double bottoms of the ships. And we worked ten hours a day, five days a week. Since we were women we couldn't work on the gravy days—on Saturday and Sunday. And I liked my work. I couldn't do it at first and they almost threw me out. I couldn't do the first striking; I'd go straight down. . . . Finally, I said to this guy—the snapper—I said, "Scotty, let me try that second step." He said, "You can't do the first step, how can you do the second?" I said, "Would you let me try?" So I got this thing set up and I was trying to strike an arc and nothing was happening, and he said, "Ground." So I took the thing off and put it on the ground. That's to show you how dumb I was! So we got that straightened out and I struck an

arc and I was able to do that right then, and I was one of their best welders . . .

Joan, age seventy, is still working and believes she will probably continue to do so. Although she would like to be able to retire, Joan has worked since she was a teenager, and it is very much a part of who she is. A sense of pride was evident when Joan talked about what she has done.

> I look back and I think, yeah I worked for [a factory], I worked for the shipyards, drove a school bus, I owned a tavern, ran an auto parts store for my parents for a while. . . . I've either owned my own business or I've worked in an element that you could wear your jeans and your boots and just be who you are. . . . [When] I owned a tavern, we had a lot of women come in. A lot of the feminist movement did, and that was exciting. . . . [It was a challenge] to make a bar—a rundown straight bar—to change it into a women's bar. I've always pretty much enjoyed my work. I've done a lot of jobs. . . .

Ellen, at sixty-two, is now working part-time. Like so many of the women, she thoroughly enjoyed her work. Her time in the military gave her a great sense of accomplishment.

> I joined the [military] in 1952. . . . I enjoyed my time in the [military]. I was a meteorologist, that was kind of neat. . . . We were ninety-two to ninety-five percent accurate in forecasting. And we didn't have all these instruments. I enjoyed that time. . . . When I went into the [military], I was the first one that ever got both of the medals that go out at the end of boot camp. Every year the women pick one and the officers and crew pick another and I got both of them for the first time. . . . I like to accomplish a lot. I don't have that competitive thing anymore. It's rubbed off, thank goodness, because of wearing me out.

PLANNING FOR RETIREMENT

Many of the women were able to retire with enough money to be comfortable. For others, however, financial security was a struggle—

both while they worked and after. Many of the women were professionals, i.e., lawyers, psychologists, teachers, counselors, managers, and the like. But they, like their counterparts in blue- or pink-collar jobs, earned less than the men in the same jobs did. The call of "equal pay for equal work" came long after many had already left the workforce, thus, leaving them financially more vulnerable. Their concerns about their futures once they retired were quite valid.

Catherine grew up poor in a family marked by alcoholism. "I'm a former Catholic, Irish from Boston, Democrat, Liberal . . . I do jokingly refer to myself as a recovering Irish Catholic." At age sixty-three, Catherine still works full-time and recognizes that she probably will need to continue to work past sixty-five. She tries not to worry about having enough money for retirement.

> I would like not to have to work so hard when I'm sixty-five, which is only two years from now, and maybe work three days a week. I don't know if I can. I may not be able to. I may have to keep working full-time. Luckily I get five weeks' vacation so that's good. But it's hard to do what I'm doing—it's so crisis oriented. That's draining. There's a part of me that's worried and there's a part of me that says you'll figure out something. You've never starved, you've always worked, and you've taken care of yourself. I do have kids. I don't really want to go live with my children but if worse comes to worst. Maybe they could build a mother-in-law . . . I'm making plans, doing what I can, but other than that, I'm not going to dwell on it. Just have to do what I can each day, and buy my lottery ticket. . . . I took eight years off when I didn't work, so that lowers your Social Security. I never made that much money when I did work. . . . I suppose it was fairly decent but women just didn't make that much in my time unless you were a professional woman, and even teachers didn't make that much.

Some women felt unprepared financially for retirement. Jean is self-employed in the building trades. She is very concerned about her financial future, as she is fifty-six and still doing physical labor. She feels she has less physical energy now, and she does not have any financial plans.

Well, I have an aunt who will probably die in . . . not too many years and I'm her remaining relative . . . and I know that she will probably leave the house to me, which will help. . . . There's some way in which I think I plan to keep on painting. I love to do things with my hands and I always dream of being able to make some money by my hands. . . . But I don't think that's very realistic. . . . It's not a plan. I don't have a real plan. I bury my head in the sand. . . . I would like to look forward to being able to retire. And I admit I feel envious of people who have retirement plans, and I don't know how to figure it out for myself. I mean, if I could retire, my life would be at least as full as it is now.

Mary Alice was devastated when she was let go from her job—a job she planned to retire from. She had never really given much thought to retiring. In fact, she never thought about it. Material acquisitions and the amount of money she made were the main issues. It was only when her financial circumstances changed that she gave any thought to how, at fifty-eight, she was going to continue to support herself.

I used to think it was important to have a lot of stuff and to be able to say how much money I made. . . . I spent a lot of money; I didn't enjoy it. I have a totally different attitude toward money now and I do fine. I'd like to say that it was not due to circumstances but it was. When I lost my job, my last job, I was making too much money to be continued there and so I was replaced by three people, later on, and that was a terrible blow to me. My plan was to just continue to work there forever. . . . So I just went out and did some freelance work for a few more years and took early retirement—Social Security. And that's where I am. And I have managed to make it work. . . . With this new direction in my life . . . earning a little money [I'll] feel a little more comfortable, a little secure. When that occurs, I think I'll be just fine being alone. Before . . . the only thing important to me was to find a partner, someone to share my life with. I did not want to grow old alone. [Now] I feel just fine.

Subsequently, Mary Alice returned to school. At age sixty-eight, she is looking forward, within a year, to beginning a new career.

Those who worked in the home for many years faced a different set of circumstances. For example, Teresa, age sixty-seven, married and had children even though she knew she was lesbian. During this time she also had a number of lesbian relationships. She delayed getting divorced from her husband in order to be better off financially. Long after she and her husband were separated and even after her children were grown, she continued to stay married.

> The longer I stayed married, the more his retirement fund grew and I would get half of it. It was very crass. But I did it consciously because I knew that as we age, we need funds and I think that is the saddest thing about many lesbians I know now, who left their husbands with just the clothes on their backs and didn't stick around long enough to cross the Ts and dot the Is, get all the things in order, so they're suffering greatly now. And I think that's—those of us who weren't employed probably raised children and reentered the workforce at a real disadvantage, and income-wise we were very low on the totem pole because we were twenty-five years late getting in there. . . . And therefore our entry-level salaries were—we could never catch up with all those women who started out at the beginning, at college or high school [and continued in the workforce].

RETIREMENT

Retirement had different meanings for the women. For some it meant freedom to do what they wanted, to be more open, to be who they are. Donna, age seventy-one, is active and involved. She believes that since her family is long-lived she will be active for some time to come. She does, however, look at retirement with some ambivalence.

> I think the question is, why now that I'm retired don't I have the courage to be totally who I am? . . . Politically I keep hearing the more of us that are out, the easier it is for all of us. I buy that. I think that's great, but for me personally . . . I guess I'm out to anybody who wants to know because I don't have a job. Doesn't matter you know.

Other women looked forward to the increased leisure time that comes with retirement. At fifty-five, Frances reflected on her desire to retire and pursue her passions. She expressed her high hopes for retirement.

> [A]s long as I'm comfortable, I don't need a lot of money, I don't need to be rich. I just need to be able to pay my bills—pay my rent, food, and play golf. I love to play golf. . . . I want to retire. I really do. . . . Then I can play golf as much as I want . . . I love it. I truly look forward to retirement. I'll never be bored. I will always have something to do. I love to work outside and I love to be active. I love to read. I'll never be lonely because I'm an outgoing person and I'll always have people to support me. I really feel that.

A few women planned to work indefinitely and did not consider retirement a pleasing prospect. Amy described herself as having had lots of family support for "believing I could do anything I wanted." She came out when she was nineteen, stayed out, and "never lost a job because I was a lesbian either—even way back then." At age sixty-two, with a partner more than ten years younger than she, Amy is not interested in retirement.

> My dad worked until he was eighty-two, and the concept of retiring doesn't really appeal to me. I like to work and I bet you that I'll work for quite a while. And fortunately I'm healthy so I'm not looking toward retirement with bated breath. In fact, I'll probably work a long time.

Those women who had retired were far from idle. They did not find retirement something to dread, as did Amy. Some did volunteer work, others took a part-time job, and still others relished having more time to enjoy their partners, projects, and leisure activities. Teresa described the meaning of her volunteer work with people living with AIDS.

> I'm lucky. I'm extremely fortunate . . . I think being age sixty-eight is delicious. I've been around the block a few times and I don't stand for much crap. I'm lucky enough to be retired and I get to do volunteer work that I believe in and I'm an AIDS ac-

tivist for sure. . . . I like to think of myself as a student and as a spiritual person and as a person who tries to have their oar in the water and try to keep things going. Do my part; I guess that's a good way to say it.

Susan, age fifty-six, continued to work part-time after she retired. Early retirement allowed her to be to be fully out. She currently is pursuing a career as a writer.

[T]he day I turned fifty was the day I retired, and twelve days [later] I was on a plane over to Europe to start a new adventure. And so fifty for me was a wonderful release. It meant that I was free of working for the state and being a slave to them and that I could go out and have some adventures that I'd never in my life been able to afford to do before. . . . Now I work about half-time and I love not having to go to work every day.

Although retirement could be a time of stress, especially if health or financial problems existed, most found that it opened opportunities for travel, for education, and most important for the appreciation of family, friends, and partners. Most of the women did not sorely miss their work. Barbara and her partner of eighteen years retired at about the same time and discovered that retirement had benefits that work did not: "[I]t's getting better with age and with retirement we can do the things we love to do together and we can travel and appreciate each other in our lives. And each day is a wonderful new beginning."

Chapter 5

Aging and Hopes for the Future

I think old age is a marvelous time of life . . . and I feel like I'm going to keep on as long as I live. I don't have any fears of growing old; I am old. And I'm happy about that.

Kay, age seventy-one

Aging and old age are relative concepts. What is considered "old age" is dependent upon the century and era in which one was born. Historically, life expectancy was short, infant mortality was high, and poor nutrition, accidents, rudimentary medicine, and diseases of epidemic proportions ensured that the life span remained relatively short. By the mid-1800s a growing middle class, better access to food, improved medical care, and health education efforts began to reduce mortality rates for children and adults. But it was not until after World War I, and the subsequent advances in medicine and technology, that old age and the social concepts that we now associate with aging emerged.

In 1789 life expectancy in the United States for males was 34.5 years and for females, 36.5 years. By 1897 it was 44.09 for males and 46.61 for females. By 1929 it had risen to 58.11 and 61.36 respectively for males and females. Now, at the beginning of the twenty-first century, the proportion of the population that is sixty-five and older is projected to rise to more than 20 percent of the population by 2040. The proportion that is eighty-five and older is growing especially quickly, more rapidly than any other segment of the population. As life expectancy increases, age-related experiences and concerns change.

We asked the women in this study about their own experiences as they age, their anticipations about growing older as well as their concerns and their hopes for the future. In response to our questions, the women reflected upon their lives, where they are today, what they might face in the future, and the advice they would offer to others. They shared their journeys in relation to their own aging and the challenges they face, particularly in relation to physical health, cognitive abilities, maintaining independence, and potential care and housing needs. They expressed their anticipations and worries about having sufficient resources for their later years as well as about their physical limitations, their relationships, and their mortality. Many of the women also discussed their hopes for the future, offering a glimpse of the importance of their dreams. They shared their deep satisfaction with their lives and some of the joys of aging. For some, being old meant finally having the freedom to be themselves. For others, aging meant basking in the security of a long, lasting love relationship—but knowing it too must end.

AGING: THE CHALLENGES AND ANTICIPATIONS

These lesbian elders expressed a variety of attitudes about growing old. Although some acknowledged the physical limitations they face as they age, many said that what mattered most was how they felt inside. In any event, they looked forward to living active, full lives.

At seventy-one, Edith views aging as a process that is part of her: Her body is growing older while her inner self remains young. She was very agile during her younger years, but now her increased limitations are becoming noticeable.

> Well, I'm daily surprised that I'm seventy-one years old. It seems like—I think often of my father-in-law at age ninety—and he said to me that, "You know, outside I'm old, but inside I don't feel much different than I did when I was fourteen." And I'm beginning to understand what he was saying better and better as the years go by, because so much inside doesn't change, while the outside changes quite noticeably. . . . But I think having been healthy all my life, I'm probably afraid of having a painful end or a painful disease or something like that, and I'm not real sure about death, what that's going to be. That's sort of scary. But I also think that a lot of the clichés about getting old are a bunch of nonsense. I mean, you hear about all the difficult things and the hard things and the diseases and the infir-

mities and so on. And certainly, I have arthritis and it's inca-
pacitating sometimes. . . . But at the same time, if I can still
manage to totter around—we're within walking distance of
town and the grocery store and the library and those things. And
my night vision for driving at night is lessening—so those kinds
of things. And yet at the same time some of the things that I have
thought I always wanted to do are becoming less important, so it
doesn't matter quite so much if I'm not as mobile or independent as I have been—I don't need to be. So, it's an adventure.

At eighty-two, Shirley has not experienced the physical limitations
that go along with illness. She is still working as a surveyor and has
no intention of becoming ill. She attributed her good health to her attitude and her religious beliefs.

I'm not going to get sick. It isn't necessary. The reason we get
sick as we get older is because we expect to. We are conditioned
to. And everything we see on television, everything you hear on
radio, everything you read in the newspaper—you've got to get
ready because you're going to be sick. . . . You just don't have to
believe it.

Being seventy-five has not caused Ernestine to slow down either.
She is active in many volunteer organizations and believes that being
involved and helping people keeps her young. "I don't consider age.
[I'm] seventy-five and I'm going to tell them that I am fifty-seven.
They'll know that is not true. It's just a reversal of seventy-five."

In general, the women were enjoying their lives and looked forward to growing older. After various careers in the art field, Sally, at
sixty-nine, is as interested in life as ever. Content and even glad to be
at this point in her life, she defined "elderly" as seventy and above.

[At] seventy you're getting elderly. But I'm sort of looking forward to [it]. I'm more now with my art than I've ever done before, on a consistent level, and of course being retired I have
time, but also impetus to do it. I just think life is so fascinating
and there is so much stuff out there to be interested in. I don't see
my interest lagging in anything.

Kate, at sixty-one, is almost a decade away from Sally's definition of elderly. Very athletic when she was young, she is still very physically active and looks forward to "a simple life" with her long-term partner after retirement.

> I'm sixty-one years old, and the things that I look forward to are hoping my body's holding up. . . . Hopefully, my mind will stay sharp during that period of time. . . . I look forward to actually being able to retire, to do a little traveling, although I'm a big home person. . . . My home is very important to me. . . . I want my body to stay together enough that I can still go out and putter around and plant things, that sort of thing.

Though many of the women did not see themselves as old, society treated them as such. Some discussed the cultural realities of aging, instances of age discrimination, and their awareness of the ageist nature of our society. A number mentioned one very real obstacle they encountered, namely ageism. For example, they noted the ready acceptance by society, young and old, of greeting cards that under the guise of humor, depict the elderly as physical and/or mental buffoons—or worse.

Kay is seventy-one. She and her partner were prepared for the vicissitudes that often accompany aging; for example, she and her partner have taken financial and legal steps to ensure their independence and well-being. Kay looks forward to devoting more time to combating ageism within the lesbian community. She noted that her experience of aging differs dramatically from society's stereotypes about growing old.

> I think there is a lot of ageism in this [lesbian] community. I think [my partner] and I have managed to bridge the gap somewhat by being actively involved in these groups of people that include women of all ages, and I think we're trying to combat this ageism, trying to convince people that just because you're old doesn't mean you're incompetent and incapable, worn out, or passed out. We're not. And I think old age is a marvelous time of life. I've worked all my life and enjoyed my life and enjoyed my work, but now I'm enjoying the retirement even more than I've ever enjoyed working, and I feel like I'm going to keep on

as long as I live. I don't have any fears about growing old; I am old. And I'm happy about that.

FINANCIAL SECURITY

For many of the women, financial security was crucial in maintaining independence—an issue of paramount interest to them as they approach the demographic designation of old age. Inequality in the workplace, i.e., gender-based discrimination that limited promotional and financial opportunities, meant that retirement and the quality of retirement could be precarious at best. Those in their fifties—younger women in terms of the age range of those interviewed—seemed particularly concerned about having the financial resources to see them through. A more general concern, expressed by women of various ages, was ensuring that their wishes would be carried out in the event of their illness or death. To that end, most of the women, whatever their financial situation, had prepared the necessary legal documents.

Elaine is single and works for a nonprofit agency. Although she has made some moves toward financial planning, at fifty-seven, she worries about her future finances.

> Well, I work at an agency that doesn't have a retirement plan and I worry about that a little bit. Some years ago I invested in mutual funds; I have an IRA account, my own personal savings plan. A lot of the money I earn as a therapist I'm putting away toward older age. . . . My two sisters and I talk about in the future—they're both married—that when the husbands are gone, maybe we're all going to live together. I don't know that that's going to be a reality, but we talk about it so that we can pool our resources and look ahead to that. I'm not overly concerned about it, but I am aging and I think, whoa, am I going to have enough cushion when I get there? So it's something that's on my mind.

Judy, at fifty-seven, has not yet worked the twenty years of service required for full pension at her job. She has given much thought to what she and her partner will need to do to remain financially independent when they retire.

Well, I think both of us carry with us what probably all women have and that is a fear of becoming a bag lady. . . . All the women I know harbor and will admit to harboring a fear of becoming a bag lady. I think that's why Lily Tomlin's thing was so effective. And my hope is that I will be sufficiently secure by the time I retire that I won't become a bag lady. That's my hope. Now I don't have anybody—I have no children so I don't have anybody to worry about after me. . . . My goal is to come out even . . . I have—I'm a state employee. Now I do not have a lot of years as a state employee so that by the time . . . I will have about twenty years by the time I've retired . . . so presumably I'll end up with about 40 percent of my salary. That's not enough to live on. . . . What I would like is for us to have sufficient income from something like rental property . . . something that would grow with inflation.

Her partner Beth, fifty-five years old, has a more positive assessment of how they will fare.

[We] have done documents, powers of attorney and that sort of thing. We've acquired property. I have rental property in LA and we have some up here. So, we are counting on that as a way to provide . . . for the future. . . . We talked a lot at one point [with friends]; we were thinking if we could go together and buy property together, we could live next door and support one another.

At seventy, Joan is retired and sees herself as not well-off but financially "comfortable." She has given considerable thought to the realities of being female, lesbian, and aging.

So I think financing of course is a real big problem for lesbian women. The older ones in my bracket, a lot of them have not had the jobs, and they don't have the financial. . . . Women are getting a little more money now than we used to get. I was fortunate here again, when I worked at [a factory], I got paid the same [as men].

Like Joan, Nancy, age sixty-two, also benefited from working in a nontraditional job for women. After thirty years in manufacturing, she retired with good benefits and feels quite secure—as much as one can—about the future.

> We both have a will. . . . We have put my 401(k) from [employer] in an investment plan. We have a straight woman who does investments for some lesbian friends of ours. . . . She doesn't question our relationship, but obviously must know. . . . I was very adamant . . . that all my money would go to my partner. All our accounts are in both our names.

Kay believed that she had prepared well and neither she nor her partner needed to worry. They have considered the possibility of assets remaining after both of their deaths and what they want to have happen to those resources.

> What we've done about [finances] is that I have it covered legally so that I have the power of attorney and all these things are taken care of legally. Economically, I think I'm in a position— I live in a home that's paid for and I have rental income that's paid for my rental properties [and they are] paid for. And I have money that comes in. I have enough money probably to pay for whatever help I might need. Now and in the future. And my partner does too, so I don't think we would be economically dependent on anyone . . . if one or the other will die first, the remaining one will have the property and income until—as long as they survive, then it goes to a lesbian [fund].

INDEPENDENCE AND DEPENDENCE

Certainly, many of the women spoke to the challenges associated with aging. With aging they faced numerous changes—both losses and gains—as they balanced maintaining their own independence while reaching out and accepting new levels of support from and dependence on others. The women's experiences of aging depended on health, financial resources, and frame of mind—along with various other factors that can impact old age. The ability to maintain good health—and avoid disability—was a primary concern for the majority of the women.

The possibility of being alone and dependent on others for help was of great concern to the women, whether they had family or not. Laura, at fifty-seven, with children and grandchildren, is in a long-term relationship and still working, yet she has thought a lot about growing older.

> One of the things that I concern myself about getting older is . . . being by myself. And that's always been a concern of mine, and I don't want to live with my children just because I'm older. I'd like to be able to live with others who are older who are like me. And so that is one of my major concerns about getting older. Number one, losing my health, losing my ability to think and do things that I can—I don't want to be laying crippled or crazy as I get older, and those are concerns of mine. I would like to have— I would not necessarily have to have the full facility of my limbs if I could still operate a vehicle or drive one of those three-wheeled bicycles, not be dependent. I want to be ambulatory. And I also want to have my senses. But I don't want to be by myself.

At sixty-nine, Sally lives alone and is in fairly good health. However, her experience with her mother's aging, has left her with concerns about her future.

> I think the one thing I'm a little concerned about in the future is—couples aren't this concerned about it because they always think they'll have the other one to take care of them when they're older and can't do things themselves. I had my mother who went into a rest home. And I think I probably am concerned—number one with the future is how am I going to handle really getting old and not being able to take care of myself? My mother lived to be eighty-eight, but the last few years were pretty shitty. If she hadn't had money, I don't know where she would have been. . . . The biggest concern I have is where is the final type of life going to be and what's it going to be like?

Other women echoed Sally's concern about the final stage of life and expressed a desire to maintain some independence and control over how they die as well as how they live. Ninety-five-year-old Madelyn is dealing directly with the difficulties of aging with dignity.

She and her partner of fifty-eight years had bought into a multicare retirement community, and they were, at this point, in the nursing home section—together in the same room. Except for the previous few months, they had lived completely closeted. Because of her partner's increased dementia and her own deteriorating physical condition with its potential for mental deterioration, Madelyn had twice attempted suicide. She came to realize that suicide is not the answer, but firmly believes that the loss of independence is a loss of dignity and power. In order to maintain independence and thus, dignity, Madelyn said she needed "to be involved to have some reason to live. Be working on something like what I'm working on now."

> My only concern is to try to die with dignity and not sit here and have it chipped away. . . . The right to die, that's the major concern now because there is no other concern that is going to affect us in any way but the ability to die with dignity and have the right of choice in your life. . . . I'd love to go right now because I still can go with dignity, and pretty soon you get to the bedpan stage. And you can feel your powers being chipped away as you sit there. It's an awful feeling. Just watch yourself deteriorate. It's cruel. Losing everything. Because when you lose your strength, your mind too is affected. And it is amazing how you know that. You can see it; you can feel it, every day.

HOUSING AND COMMUNITY

Most of the women hoped to remain in their own homes until the very end. However, they were realistically concerned that physical or mental deterioration would lead to a loss of independence and perhaps an eventual need for care in an assisted-living facility or nursing home. They certainly hoped to avoid nursing homes. However, acknowledging that health and circumstances might require such a move, a number of women expressed the desire for an assisted-living facility or nursing home specifically for lesbians. Their reasons for wanting a home for lesbians included the desire to be with other lesbians, to feel safe, and to have choices.

Julie, at fifty-nine, is discovering the need to adapt to some physical limitations as she grows older. She worries that she and her partner may not be physically able to continue caring for and living in their current home, a house in the country that they built themselves when they were younger. She hopes that their group of lesbian friends can help one another with home repairs, maintenance, and upkeep.

> I didn't know the body sort of gave up on you like it does! That was a real shock, I think, to realize that in my head and my mind I want to continue doing—we have this big house and this big property and we just planned to stay here at least until we retire. Well, we're both now not able to do all the things we used to do. We helped build this house, we did all the inside painting, we've painted the outside of it . . . and just so many jobs like that that we just did. Our group of friends would get together and we'd do it like when we built the house—everybody came over and built the back deck together and all that. And we can't do that anymore, as a rule. We're not able to. And that's one of the things—I think my major concerns about the future have to do with physical. And neither [of us] are people who sit around and worry about getting this disease or that disease, but . . . I have an eye condition that means I'm going to probably lose my vision earlier, and right now I'm having a lot of trouble with my driving so I think if I got to the point where I can't drive, what are we going to do out here? Do we have to move into town, which neither one of us wants to do? Those are the kinds of things I think that concern me as much as anything.

Maria, age sixty-three, is concerned that she may not be able to continue living alone because of increased costs for health care and medicine for her arthritis. Without the financial resources to pay for services such as nursing care or physical therapy, she will not be physically capable of living alone and sees no option but a nursing home.

> The biggest concern I guess is physically. A couple of years ago, when I first came down with arthritis and Western medicine wasn't getting me anywhere and I actually was about as capable of walking then as I am now, it looked to me like I was going to end up in a nursing home. . . . But it was—I was either going to make money, enough to be able to hire a nurse to come and take care of me, or I wouldn't make any money and I'd end up in a nursing home and I'd die anyway. So now, my concern is, will I

be able to continue living alone? But it's not just the living alone, it's being able to do things. And that's my biggest concern. It's like today—what the hell am I going to do about dinner?

Amy, age sixty-two, is currently in a fifteen-year relationship she described as happy. She expressed the desire to choose with whom to spend her last years.

Let's say that we really were unable to stay in this house because we were elderly to the point that we needed managed care or something. I would really like to see us be able to go to a place that was a lesbian place. . . . I certainly prefer lesbians' company to anybody else's, period. Now that doesn't mean that I think all heterosexuals are awful. I don't think that at all, and I do have some heterosexual friends, but if I'm going make a choice, I'm going to have the lesbians around me.

At sixty-four, Christine is still working as a bus driver and is well aware of the aging population as she "sees them in varying degrees of mobility and capability." Although she doesn't envision being ready for a nursing home anytime soon, she would, if older, want to be in a lesbian nursing home.

I'm certainly aware of my own mortality. And I would like to see a rest home for lesbians to die with some dignity and together. Although I have no desire to live just primarily among lesbians, I know some gals do that. I think I'd be missing a lot in my life if I did that. But in my older life, or older-older—say I can't get around anymore—I'd like to die in a home with lesbians.

Many of the women cited community as a reason to live with other older lesbians as they age. Thinking back to her experiences in a commune during the 1960s, Donna, now seventy-one, believes a communal arrangement of some kind would provide an alternative to standard assisted-living or nursing homes, which tend to be blind to the needs of aging lesbians.

I think I would like to be in a community of women, probably lesbian women, if I had to be in a nursing home or retirement home. . . . That has been a sort of dream of mine for many, many years—to have a community. And many of my friends say, "Oh, I don't know what I'm going to do." I say, "Well, let's get a great big house and we'll help each other." I've always thought that. And I have lived in communities.

Not all the women saw lesbian care facilities as being a desirable solution. Kay believes that old age is relative and that many of the problems associated with aging can be taken care of by means other than assisted-living or nursing homes—lesbian or otherwise. At seventy-one, she is actively involved in aging issues, and is working with other lesbians to establish an in-home care agency for lesbians by lesbians.

[T]his would provide employment for some of the younger women—part-time employment for some of those who are still in school—and provide support services, financial, emotional, legal, and economic help to enable old people who become disabled to stay in their homes—provided they have homes. And if they don't, then we have an idea that we could probably put people together, where if somebody has a home and is really old— I'm thinking in their nineties. . . . Home sharing and a home-care thing so that if people became terminally ill, they would not have to be shipped off to a straight nursing home.

At sixty-six Phyllis and her partner have begun looking ahead to the coming years. In making plans, she has considered her desire for community in old age, and she offered another alternative to lesbian-only nursing homes.

We really need to sit down and look at where we are, our health and our concerns, and say, "Can we obligate ourselves here for another few years? Does it look feasible?" I mean, don't wait until they have to pull us off the place—we don't want that. I have a concern that if anything should happen to [my partner] in growing older—of being isolated from the gay community. . . . This really worries me, the isolation. . . . It would be nice if you needed a facility, if you could call the gay hotline [to learn what] places are gay friendly. Because if you were going to have to be in some sort of care center, it would certainly be nice if you knew the ones that you should be in.

Obviously, the lesbian care facility and its variations, although not at this time a real option, was for many lesbians a subject of some importance and discussion. For others, it was simply not a consideration either because they did not consider it realistic or desirable, or because their focus was on financially securing the ability to remain at home. Many women simply made other plans as they became aware of their increasing dependence on others, such as buying a smaller place, moving to an apartment, hiring help, or making arrangements for mutual caretaking.

Madelyn and her partner didn't have the option of a lesbian facility when they moved into their multicare retirement center. Now in the skilled-nursing section of the facility, Madelyn reflected on "blending" at her current living situation.

> [T]hen even in coming here [to the retirement center], we came in here and there was no question in our minds that they would question us, and they didn't. And we said we wanted an apartment with a bedroom and so on, and they said we've got a beautiful apartment and showed it to us and we took it, and from that time on it was just blending all the time. . . . You'd think that they would question these two women wanting this apartment— I thought at the time—no I didn't, it never occurred to me. It just went by. But I was lucky in that earlier period, where I don't think there was much known about . . . homosexuals, really. Nobody was talking about it, so we weren't talking about it.

Some of the women preferred not to spend their later years exclusively with other old people. Now seventy, Margery expressed her preference to be with younger people very directly.

> I don't like being around groups of old people. I don't like the energy, even though I'm part of them. I like a lot of old people individually. . . . I don't want to live in a retirement community. I don't want to be around all those old people.

Although not directly ruling out retirement or nursing homes— lesbian or otherwise—Barbara, who is sixty-nine, made it clear that such living arrangements were not high on her list. In point of fact, she planned to avoid them, if at all possible.

> I want to keep on doing and being as long as I can comfortably. . . . Unless you go out of your way to keep younger friends and to keep a younger attitude about what you do and who you are— I'm sure that I could be isolated if I really wanted to be, but I wouldn't ever want to be. I'm sure that I could make friends of only my doddering old age group if that was what I felt comfortable with. But I would rather have younger friends because I'm going to need them when I can't struggle on my own. So I'm going to keep generating my younger friends as much as I possibly can.

PARTNERSHIPS:
JOURNEYING THROUGH LIFE TOGETHER

Most of the women, whether they currently are partnered or not, spoke of their hopes of being able to grow old sharing their declining years with a beloved partner. The benefits they cited were many (and no different from those for heterosexuals) including having two incomes instead of one, emotional stability, less isolation, the ability to help each other cope with health problems, and more important, the sharing of discovery of life's journey.

Ann anticipates growing old within the context of a deep love relationship. Her relationship with her life partner embraces mutuality, affection, sexuality, spirituality, adventure, and security. She shared her expectations about growing old with her partner.

> I anticipate that the two of us will grow old together. And I anticipate that we will always find something to bring joy to our lives because I think this is—I can't imagine people who say, "Oh, how do you stand not working, aren't you bored?" We're never bored. We always—there's always something that we are involved with, and so while I hope that we can [be] physically active as long as possible and we try to look after our health so that we can try to make that possible—that we can help spiritually, make that happen for us in our bodies. I think that we will probably always find joy along the way. We're both, I think we're both

at the point and so even if we reach that point that we can't get out and walk our three miles every day, which I hope we can keep doing until we're at least 100, that we can sit together and enjoy the view and play gin rummy! So, I guess I have a very positive outlook about our growing old together.

Laura, who is fifty-seven, has been in a relationship with her partner for the past twenty-one years. She described how her sense of aging is also tied to "growing old together" and to pursuing her own dreams.

My ideal of what I wanted when I got older was to be able to sit down with a partner, someone that you're planning a life with, and grow gracefully together, reminisce about the past, prepare—I'd like to write, and I would like to be with someone who has—they wouldn't have to write, they don't have to have any of those pieces, but support me in what I was doing and sitting on a rocking porch and rock. I always have ideas that that's what I can do in a relationship, just grow old together and be able to enjoy life together. Not asking for the world, just a piece of paradise.

Many of the younger women hoped that life would remain somewhat as it was at present, most having good partnerships and family relationships, relatively good health, a good home, enough financial security to meet needs, a sense of independence, and the ability to pursue their dreams.

Denise, at fifty-seven, believed that if she and her partner could maintain their current circumstances through the coming years, they will be all right into old age.

I think I look forward most to just having my life be a whole lot as it is right now because I enjoy it so much. Just to be able to be independent, to have each other, to do the things that we enjoy every day, to have enough money, which we're very good at living on small, so you know, we ought to. And those are the things that I look forward to. And to continue to see friends and to continue the good relationship that we have.

Given the strength of these women's partnerships, it is not surprising that the death of a partner was exceptionally painful. The long years of shared support, sadness, guilt, joys, rewards, and love they had experienced made this loss especially difficult. Pat, at sixty-nine, summed up the sense of sadness and the desire to keep on living: "I'm in a lonely place stage although I have a lot of straight friends—more straight than gay. I travel a lot. I have a good life. But I don't think any of us like being alone in our old age." These women are survivors. They needed to be to survive through periods of extreme homophobia, sexism, and ageism; and they continue to look to the future.

HOPES FOR THE FUTURE

Overall, the women were settled and satisfied with their lives, and when they were asked about their life regrets, they had relatively few. Some of the women did share that some of the important relationships in their life remained unresolved, and others wished they had prepared more for old age, traveled more, or taken more risks. For example, fifty-six-year-old Jean expressed that she wished she had a pension, as well as the ability to make her dreams a reality.

> I've thought about starting [a group] for a long time and I've never quite made it happen . . . a small group, like five women, that would really take each other on, and it would be a group where you could go, saying this is something I want to do and I'm feeling stuck and I need some help thinking about how to make it happen. That's a big thing I would change. . . . I think another thing that I would like to change would be the areas where I feel hopeless about myself particularly. The areas where I get stuck and confused and just, you know, hopelessness, year after year. Those are the things I would change.

When asked about what they would change in their lives, the women shared both their disappointments as well as their visions and dreams for the future. Some wished they could provide more security for themselves and their families, and others wished that the world were a more peaceful and just place.

Amy, age sixty-two, and a retired professional, talked about her dream of finishing a long-held goal: writing a novel.

Well, one thing I would really like to do before I die is write a book. But I've got lots of publications, it's not that—I'm not interested in having my name last for posterity. Been there, done that. But I think that I could write some of these novels a lot better than the people who write them, and I'd like to do that, and I don't have time. And I'd also like to be a lot better, have a lot more facility with my computer, but I'll achieve that. I'm not worried about that; I know I'll achieve that. But you know, my life is really very good.

Other women expressed how they wished they could make an impact beyond their own individual lives. Teresa, at sixty-eight, cited many things of which she is proud, including the raising of her two children, her relationship with her partner, and who she has become as a woman. She expressed a wish for increased openness about being gay. "Do away with all homophobia. . . . Do away with all homophobia and AIDS. To make it all right for us to have lived openly, that would have been the best thing. The very best thing."

Ellen took Teresa's idea even further. At sixty-two, she acknowledged that such a change "would mean changing the whole world."

And that would be being accepted as normal people. Just to be able to be yourself wherever you were, and walk down the streets and hold hands—such a simple thing. It would be tolerance. I would wave the wand for tolerance, and peace, and love.

Chapter 6

Adversity

[My partner] was diagnosed with lung cancer and she only had three months to live. The one thing we did do was lie and indicate that we were sisters. . . . You stay out there on the outside [of the hospital] looking in unless you tell a lie to get in.

Helen, age seventy-three

Throughout life people embrace times of triumph and times of challenge. The politics of the era, the norms of family and community, and the inner strengths of each person all influence the impact of life experiences. The women in this study lived through the Great Depression, World War II, the McCarthy era, the social revolution of the 1960s, and, now, the turn of the century. As we have seen, the political and social environment in which these women came of age was difficult at best, given the extent of various types of oppression. From the 1920s though the 1950s, all women contended with cultural mores that narrowly defined them and their place and role in society. Except for the brief period during World War II when they were needed in the factories, women were expected to fulfill their designated role as wives and mothers. Job opportunities were limited and the social pressures to conform were repressive, isolating, and often destructive. For women of color, the situation was compounded by segregation, violence, and the absence of legal protection against racial discrimination. During this same period, severe antigay activities were also taking place. These included the medicalization and pathologizing of same-sex relationships, military interrogations, discrimination in the workplace, bashings at the local bars, and the lack of protection from law enforcement to name a few. Some lost their jobs or their children and some experienced involuntary hospitalizations or lobotomies. This atmosphere had an immense effect on the women's lives and their decisions. Many lesbians sought to protect themselves by going underground and remaining invisible. By repressing and hiding their sexual orientation, they passed in heterosexual society but they often paid a heavy price.

The women in this study were the witnesses and the survivors. A number of them had grappled with alcoholism, withstood the medical profession's "cures" for homosexuality, or confronted serious health problems. These experiences most often made them stronger and more aware of their own abilities. Their stories illustrate the success of their survival and, for a few, scars so deep that true healing seemed out of reach. Often the events themselves were not most central to the women's recollections, but rather their responses—and, in most cases, their abilities to triumph in the face of great adversity.

FAMILY REJECTION

The stories in Chapter 2 on coming out illustrate the challenges and consequences for these older lesbians of disclosing their sexual orientation. Given the homophobia of the eras in which many of these women realized that they were lesbian, most never told their parents. By the time society was more forgiving, their parents were so old that many daughters saw no point in telling them. Many never talked about it to their families but assumed they knew, and everyone carried on without any confrontations. For those who did tell, some were vociferously castigated while others experienced the invalidation of having this important disclosure ignored.

Edith, age seventy-one, came out later in life after being married for twenty-eight years. When she told her mother that she was a lesbian, her mother responded by ignoring the information. As Edith talked about this experience, her attitude was one of resigned acceptance.

> And I told my mother I was lesbian, and mother's reaction to that sort of thing is to say, "Oh. Okay," and then, "How are you coming with your jigsaw puzzle?" You know. And it was never discussed again. . . . She wasn't the drop-in kind of a mother, which is probably to some degree why I am the way I am. She antagonized all of her grandchildren. I don't think I've antagonized mine, but that separation was very evident and although

she lived here in town, she never just dropped by. Never. She just recently died, as a matter of fact, and she would have been one hundred if she'd lived two more months. So she lived a long time. . . . I think when I was small and my parents were gone, I can remember saying to myself, "Well, if you don't care too much, it won't hurt quite so bad." So I think that is an attitude that became integral to me at the time and consequently there's been distance. And I don't know that my lesbianism worsened that or changed that negatively, from my point of view. Like I said, I never heard from my mother.

When Stephanie, age fifty-seven, left her husband for a woman, her relationship with her parents suffered. After a few years of no contact, she came out to her mother and confronted her about her homophobic behavior. Eventually they reconciled and Stephanie received the kind of parental support she wanted.

When I left my husband, my parents actually flew down and kind of confronted me: "What are you doing to your child? What are you doing to your husband?" And the reason for leaving was never stated, and they knew that I was close with this woman but how much they ever assumed I don't know. It was not until after my father died, probably about three years ago . . . I was essentially out of touch with them for four years mostly, and I finally saw my mother, went back to visit her when I felt I healed a lot of stuff. But just before that time, as part of that healing, I wrote a letter and said, "You know, as a Christmas present I want you to know about me." And I told her a bunch of stuff and being a lesbian was about third on the list, I think. And I took a partner back home with me, and [my mother] had some discomfort with that, would have been more comfortable if we'd stayed in separate rooms, but [we] didn't. And she would send cards just to me, and I got pissed, and I said, "You know, if my brothers were with a woman but not married or if I were with a man but not married, you'd address the cards jointly and I expect that." And eventually she started to do that and when that relationship ended, my mother actually . . . called and said how distressed she was to learn about that and was very sympathetic and loving. Said if I needed to come home to live that I was welcome.

Whether the rift with family was healed eventually, as was the case for Stephanie, or remained a painful reminder of separation, as it was for Edith, the rejection and lack of family support was painful.

One of the most heart-wrenching stories of family rejection was that of JoAnn. Now fifty-six, JoAnn was raised by a mother who fiercely wanted a little girl who would "bake cookies with her and sew and iron." Because those activities were of little interest to JoAnn, she and her mother did not get along from the very start.

> So I was a disappointment for her from the beginning and just recently I've realized that I've been a transvestite all my life. And when I was young my mother dressed me until I was twelve years old. I don't know why. I guess she thought I couldn't do it or something; it was kind of an unusual situation. But anyway, she dressed me up in dresses and she'd say, "Oh what a darling little girl you are." And I'd go crazy. I mean I would just plain go crazy, and I never knew why. And I'd go to school and I'd get through the day and I'd come home and I'd feel so guilty because of how bad I'd treated her. . . . And this went on day after day after day.

JoAnn started drinking at age nine and was heavily into drugs and alcohol all through junior high and high school. Pregnant and married at seventeen, she fell in love with a woman when she was twenty-two.

> And when my mother found out I was going to move in with this woman, she went into some kind of fit and had to be carried out of the house in a straitjacket. And she was screaming at me and my dad was screaming at me, "Look what you've done to your mother". . . . [She] told me one time that . . . in this world there were men with women, men with men, women with women, and masturbation. And she'd wished I'd masturbated. I thought that's pretty bizarre, to wish your daughter would spend her life alone masturbating. Anyway, that's really how she felt. And she thought I was always an abomination.

JoAnn had a strong dislike of her own body that seems more than the result of negative images of lesbians. She said that she'd always known that something was wrong. She had wanted to be a boy, and shared that "it was the most devastating thing in the world to me that I wasn't."

> I said [to my mother], "What do you think I am anyway?" She said, "I don't know what you are." . . . There's no way for me to tell her, you know, anyway, it upsets me. . . . I think it is wonderful that this is coming out so that maybe people can understand this a little bit more and maybe, particularly with the situation that I couldn't handle of being a girl. I mean, I just flat couldn't handle being a girl. I've never been able to—I don't—I wish I could. I have a lot of friends who are lesbians that love their bodies. You know, I hate my body. I always have. I've always hated my breasts. I hate my vagina. I hate my body. If I were young now, I guess I might even consider having some kind of surgery, although I'm too short. I'd make a funny-looking man, Charlie Chaplin or something.

Despite being in a body that "has always been uncomfortable and alien" to her, JoAnn has come to believe that she was given a female body for a purpose and that it has challenged her to grow and accept what is. She relies on her strong spiritual perspective to sustain her and get her through the day. She regrets that neither she nor her mother understood what was at the root of the fights they had when she was young. This is not surprising, as only since the 1980s has much information been available about gender identity issues, including transsexualism. Now JoAnn's mother has dementia and there is no possibility for discussion.

> So now here my mother is in a state of unconsciousness, you know, totally out of it, and I've realized what happened. And there's no way to go back, you know. There's no way to mend that. . . . But it wasn't her fault, you know? It wasn't my fault. It just was. I'm sorry she had to go through that. I'm sorry I had to go through it . . .

EDUCATION, MILITARY, AND POLITICAL LESSONS

The patriarchal society in which the women interviewed were raised devalued women in general and referred to unmarried women pejoratively as old maids and spinsters. Women who recognized their lesbianism and decided not to marry knew they needed to be better prepared and work harder than men in order to be financially independent and in order to live as they wished. One way to attain independence was to earn college and graduate degrees and thus move into professions such as law, medicine, and teaching. At a time when few women went to college and fewer yet went on to graduate school, an extraordinary number of women interviewed for this study held bachelor and graduate degrees. For most of them, education was a key. It enabled them to be independent and, most important, to develop their talents and abilities.

Sixty-two-year-old Amy described being raised by parents who believed in her. She attended all-girl schools up through high school. She believes that she benefited from the confidence she gained in such a female-only environment. Independent and an activist, Amy has no doubt that if lesbians are going to be able to support themselves, they must have a good education.

> I think the one major difference with the lesbian community—I'm not saying the gay community, I'm saying the lesbian community—that would be different than the straight community at large is that I think that there are more of us that are going to be professional than in the straight community because we have always known that we had to support ourselves. I think that was a big motivator for us, and it wasn't a motivator for a lot of people in the straight community. And I think . . . you're going to find a much higher percentage of people with professions in the lesbian [community] relative to whatever the national average is. . . . I think that if you just look around you in any group, there are an awful lot of us that are professionals. But mainly it's because we didn't care to starve to death.

Undergraduate and advanced degrees did result in economic benefits and job opportunities. But education by itself did not automatically overcome the sexist and gender rigidity of the period. A good, strong self-image was necessary to thwart the negative messages women received daily.

Donna, age seventy-one, is a retired teacher. It took her a long time to realize that one of the contributing factors to her negative self-image was her high school principal's comment on her college application.

> I think back on some of the things that I have done because my principal said—I worked in the registrar's office at my college, undergraduate college—and I saw what he [wrote] to this college, and he [wrote] to this college that [I] was not leadership material. And man, I tell you, it took me a long time to say, "Fuck you. You didn't know what you were talking about."

She spent many years with a limiting view of her capabilities and her worth. "The only things I could do was if someone else was going to be a leader." Only much later, after she received her master's degree, did she realize that she had internalized and accepted his labeling of her and that she could leave that label behind.

For many women who married young and only came to know or act on their lesbian identity later in life, supporting themselves financially was a challenge. Pat lived in the Midwest until she was fifty and then moved to the West Coast because she knew she was going to come out. She described her marriage, which took place in the early 1950s, as a time when she was completely caught up in having babies and being a housewife and mother. After twenty-four years of marriage, she divorced her husband because she recognized that the dependency in her marriage was destructive to her.

> I wanted out of the marriage and had come out and I was in a dependent state. . . . I was doing therapy, marriage therapy, and he wouldn't go. I became stronger during the therapy and I finally wanted a divorce. I insisted; he didn't want it. . . . The hardest time was figuring out with paper and pencil what I would come out with out of that marriage and deciding I can survive on that. And going to college raised my, not self-esteem, but I knew I was smart, I knew I had abilities. I was getting a 4.0 in every class. And I figured I'm going to make it out there. Between the marks at school, I knew I'd make it. As it turned out, I really had a rough time, but I made it. There were no displaced homemaker programs back then. . . . I really had to work and I survived. I was scared of that. It frightened me, but I did it. I'm proud of that.

Some of the women were able to surmount the social drawbacks of being female, lesbian, and different, and to break barriers of discrimination without degrees in higher education. Ernestine, age seventy-five, was such an individual. Her biological parents abandoned her when she was three weeks old. They left her with a neighbor couple who raised her but did not adopt her. When she was about fourteen or fifteen, her "parents" discovered she was lesbian and would no longer allow her to live with them. She then went to live with another family she knew who lived around the corner. She earned her keep while in school by stocking shelves in a grocery store. Ernestine credited her early life and work experiences for being able to overcome problems and for changing her life.

> I've always been ambitious. When I had the alcoholic parents, the foster parents, I was the one who found ways to find food. I [stocked] grocery store shelves . . . [would] earn twenty-five cents and buy ground beef . . . and make a dinner. So I've always been able to provide even when I was very young. There is no problem I cannot solve. . . . I think all the hazards I've been through have only made me stronger.

Similar to college degrees, military service often provided a means by which to rise above a homophobic, patriarchal society and build a good self-image. However, many women encountered institutionalized discrimination. Known and suspected lesbians faced witch-hunts complete with interrogations, threats, court-martials, and discharge with loss of benefits.

Kay, age seventy-one, joined the military after she divorced her first husband. During this time the military was conducting witch-hunts for homosexuals. Because Kay was dating a man, the investigators believed she was not a lesbian. In spite of the seriousness of the situation, Kay's experience with the military investigators had a humorous side that she worked to her advantage.

> I had just divorced my first husband when I went in the [military]; I was twenty. And they were having witch-hunts at that time for lesbians. They interviewed everybody, and I was so dumb, I really didn't know what one would look like if I saw one. They said, "Have you ever seen a lesbian?" I said, "I don't think so." Did I know of any? Well, of course I didn't know of

any, and I didn't think there were any in our barracks, anyway, and so—you know, I haven't seen any. The men told me that they had prostitutes coming into the men's barracks, and so I thought, well, maybe they're thinking that women are having these prostitutes that are lesbians coming into the women's barracks. So I said, "Well, I'm sure there haven't been any in our barracks, none of these lesbians there." He said, "Well, how do you know?" I said, "Well, they wouldn't be in uniform—we could recognize them." That's how dumb I was. I was a kid from a small town. I didn't know for anything about lesbians. They got such a kick out of my interview that I got called back and interviewed by some other officers. But it was the truth; I really didn't know that there might be lesbians in uniform in the [military]. But then I was going with the fellow that I later married, my second husband, and I didn't know any of the—if anyone was a lesbian, I didn't know it. I presume they were because they put some of them out and discharged them for that, but I didn't know them. So I got out of the [military] and got married again and didn't know anything about the lesbians.

Kay emerged unscathed from the military witch-hunts. Others were not so fortunate. Chapter 4 on work documents the stories of women who suffered the indignities of the interrogations as well as the consequences of discharge.

The military was not the only workplace where it was dangerous to be a lesbian. Kate, age sixty-one, is a native Californian who enlisted in the Army in order to obtain the education benefits of the GI Bill. After her tour of duty, she went to college and received a nursing degree. The time Kate spent in the military confirmed for her the importance of questioning authority, especially in righting society's wrongs. She described her life as quiet and simple, unless, as she said, "the public, society, starts jazzing us around, then I get real political."

I was once blacklisted for my political beliefs, and that was an interesting experience, and at that time I tried to sue the nurse that did that to me, and talked to an ACLU lawyer. And he wanted to take her to court and he asked me if I was willing to stand up in court and testify, "Yes, I am a lesbian but that doesn't make me a bad person or nurse." [My partner] and I were both willing to do that, and that was a lot of years ago, when it probably would have run us out of the county on a rail. . . . In order to take her [the nurse] to court, I had to have a third party who actually witnessed her slandering me. And that [witness] was quite willing to do it clear up until the day she was to go to his office and give her deposition and she chickened out. And that is understandable in a small community, a small rural community. She would have been probably blacklisted herself.

Kate did lose her job and was unable to get another nursing position for some time. She currently holds an administrative position in the medical field. She and her life partner are now politically active in their local community.

SOCIAL ISOLATION

Although nearly all of the women interviewed had rich sources of support in their lives, a few experienced painful isolation, with little or no support. A few of the women described how they became isolated later in life; others had contended with loneliness throughout their lives. Not being part of, or at least not seeing themselves as part of, the "community" because of age, lack of a partner, a tendency to embrace isolation, or any number of other reasons, caused a few of the women to feel very much alone.

Although Jean, now fifty-six, had early experiences that solidified the importance of political action as a vital source of support, she currently feels isolated. Growing up, Jean experienced the Communist Party (USA) as a dedicated political group whose members supported one another through the political witch-hunts of the 1950s. As a result, she developed a sense of political and community support as necessary to cope with a society that did not embrace those who were different, as well as to stand against oppression. Because her parents were active in the Communist Party (USA), she was ostracized, beaten up, and raped, and she often compared herself to the Rosenberg children. Consequently, as she put it, "hiding is very big in my life."

Although more than half of Jean's business is rooted in the gay/lesbian community, she is still much aware of the dangers of being labeled. As she explained, "I haven't been somebody who's come out publicly in the larger public very easily. I do it somewhat and I keep challenging myself to do it more." Jean attributed her reluctance to come out not only to homophobia but also to anti-Semitism as well as anti-communist paranoia when she was growing up.

> There have been times when it's harder to come out as a Jew than it has been to come out as a lesbian and other times when it's harder to come out as a lesbian than a Jew. . . . I see a lot of my friends either going back to church or going to church, and that's not something I see for myself. I never went to synagogue when I was a child. In my community, the spiritual one, the economic one, everything as a kid was the political one, and I think that's what I want to go back to. Those people really stayed together. And they were each other's insurance.

Jean's sense of isolation has grown as she has aged.

> I feel more and more isolation as I get older. . . . I think another part of what the isolation [is] about is the feeling of invisibility as an older lesbian. I notice it more and more often; we'll be in a room full of lesbians, and some young dyke will come up to me and say, "Are you a lesbian?" You know, it's like, have you asked anybody else in this room? No! You know, or where they just can't assume that I'm a lesbian because I look a bit older than them, and I really get offended by that. . . . I remember in [city in the East] there was a group [of older women] that was mixed—lesbian and straight. And one of the things they said to us is, "Until you begin to look at us and see us and recognize our existence, you will be as invisible as we are when you come to this place." And it was such a profound statement. I think I was in my thirties when I heard that and my friendship circles changed somewhat, but I think we are not getting that word out. And I think our different communities are very separated, a lot, whether it's race, age, economics, bar dykes, SM, or leather.

The answer to ending the isolation and growing factionalism within her different communities, Jean believes, can be found in being politically active. This was a lesson from her youth that she learned well.

> I feel a lot of isolation politically—I'm hungry to find something that I want to work on politically and I haven't found it. . . .

I'm saying in part that this whole thing about isolation is that when I worked politically I didn't feel as isolated as I do now. That political work, organizing work, was family, was community.

JoAnn did not receive early family support, and she is still in the process, at the age of fifty-six, of discovering who she is or might be. Her previous experience in acknowledging her lesbianism was very difficult: Her parents "disowned" her and she discovered that support from friends could be ephemeral.

My parents found out about it through some letters that were written from my lover. And that was a really bad situation. . . . I've come out to different friends that have rejected me for it. I've come out to friends that have accepted me for it. Been a lot of distancing.

Having experienced isolation, rejection, and loss of friendships for speaking of her lesbianism, JoAnn is reluctant to come out to others. She sees doing so as risky and frightening. Now it is only with great caution that she will bring up the subject and only to a few co-workers or longtime acquaintances. JoAnn shared that she did find some support from the gay liberation movement, which has helped her to recognize the value in being visible. However, in reality, JoAnn's search for support has led her to believe that her support comes from within.

In the past I tried to get it from other people. Now I realize that it is only within me and within my Higher Power or God or whatever it is you want to call it. And I've achieved that connection with my higher self and it's something that I can rely on completely and gets me through the day.

LOOKING TROUBLE IN THE EYE

For many of the women, coming to terms with their lesbianism and simply living their lives were stressful processes. They feared being discovered, judged, and punished by others, and often judged themselves harshly as well. Difficulties such as chemical dependency and mental health problems were often aggravated by stress. In addition, many had had or were now facing significant health problems. However, the women were not resigned to these problems: sooner or later they stood strong and tried to face them head-on.

Chemical Dependence

Understandably, alcohol and drug abuse have been a well-documented problem in the sexual minority community. For years the primary social outlets for many lesbians and gays were bars. In addition, homophobic behavior from society as well as internalized homophobia are hurtful, and drugs and alcohol have long been used to ease the pain.

Claudia, now seventy-four, used alcohol as a means to deal with "a miserable marriage" and, perhaps more important, confusion over her attraction to women. She had joined the military during World War II and developed an intense crush on another woman. It frightened her so much that she avoided the woman at all costs. After discharge she married, for the second time, and settled into the routine of a suburban housewife. Unhappy with the marriage and with herself, she started drinking.

> I was drinking mainly at home or at neighborhood parties or if we went out. I would drink, that sort of suburban drinking— neighborhood parties with straight people. There was a neighbor woman that, looking back on it, I'm pretty sure was gay. I liked her. . . . We became very close. But I think she was as confused as I was. We became very close; we had a very close friendship, but we never acted upon it in a sexual way. She had children and so did I and we did a lot of things with the kids. She drank too. So we'd drink together, kind of misery. Eventually my [husband] was transferred . . . and suddenly I was just drinking more and more, and I had a big problem. And I found my way to AA. And after two years in AA, I left my husband and then, by then I knew that I was a lesbian because I had fallen in love with my sponsor, who happened to be a gay woman, a lesbian . . .

By the time she was fifty-two, Claudia had taken control of her drinking and had become a drug and alcohol counselor. Although she did have relationships with women, she remained uncomfortable until she finally acknowledged to herself that she really was a lesbian.

I'm out there [camping and bathing in the river] and this one gal is helping me because I was shampooing my hair, and we're all out there without our clothes. And all of a sudden I thought, my God, I'm here naked with all these women. . . . Later I thought, isn't this interesting? I mean, here I am in my self-denial with all these lesbian women and they all accepted me and loved me. They were all in AA along with me, and I still didn't have a clue. I was still in denial. . . . After I retired, I called my friend and said to her, "Do you think I'm a lesbian?" She said, "My God, I can't tell you what you are. . . . Go down by the beach and sit down there and review your life, and look at yourself and examine yourself, and then figure it out." I took her advice. . . . About a month went by and I called her on the phone and said, "Guess what? I'm a lesbian." And I said, "What do I do now?" She said, "Do you want to meet some women?" and I said, "Yes!" She took me to that meeting and I felt so at home, and I've been very open ever since about who I am.

Not all of the women who were alcoholic reported a direct connection between their drinking and their lesbianism. However, sobriety was a noticeably prevalent accomplishment for many of the women interviewed. Some mentioned being a recovering alcoholic almost in passing, as a fact that was now just a part of the fabric of their lives. Others mentioned how being alcoholic had been a difficult but growth-enhancing experience.

Judy, age fifty-seven, illustrated this mixed perspective.

The most dreadful period of my life was the period of being an alcoholic. I suppose one of the things that at least I would change [if I could] would be the extent of my alcoholism because it affected my health. On the other hand, a lot of just tremendously interesting things happened to me in my life because I was an alcoholic. I ended up going to the Betty Ford [Clinic], which was a fascinating experience . . .

Unlike Judy, the other women who self-identified as alcoholic rarely received inpatient hospital treatment. AA was the primary route to their recovery. For Janet, a twelve-step program became not just a way of life, but the only way of life. After an eleven-year relationship with a married woman living in a small town, Janet moved to a large city. Following a DWI conviction, Janet recognized her "so-cial drinking" for what it really was. With prodding from her proba-tion officer, she turned to AA for help. Now, thinking positively, lik-ing herself, and making others happy are the tenets by which Janet gets through life one day at a time.

> There isn't anything in the world that could make me to take a drink. Nothing. Nothing at all. . . . I am a very positive person; I love life. I'm real fortunate that way, but I make it that way too. I don't have room for any negative [thinking] at all. Not any-where. I've always been this way pretty much, but more so since I quit drinking. I'm always happy. Oh, gosh, I've [worked] for thirty years and I still get excited when I go to work. I just love it. And I'm fortunate. I know that I am so fortunate to be where I am at in life. Oh, I'm glad I'm an alcoholic, I really am, because I wouldn't be where I am today, I don't think, if I wasn't. I don't know but it has made a better person of me. So I look back and I always remember those times and never have to go through them again.

The value of twelve-step programs was not limited to those with drinking problems. Al-Anon was instrumental in helping those whose partners or loved ones were actively alcoholic to deal with that diffi-cult circumstance. Penny, age sixty-nine, sees herself as independent and self-reliant now. She recalled a time when her former partner's drinking was a problem and she herself was sorely in need of support.

> Well, my most successful emotional support has been through Al-Anon. See, since everybody was alcoholic and [her partner] was alcoholic also it turned out. And so finally . . . I was in Cali-fornia recovering from a severe stroke with my sister. And I was complaining because [partner] was doing a lot of drinking back in Florida, and my sister . . . said, "Why don't you go to Al-Anon?" "Al-Anon, I don't need to go to Al-Anon. . . . There's nothing wrong with me, I'm not . . ." "Well," she said, "of course you are." . . . And so I did go . . . I went to Al-Anon for a while after I came up here, but then I stopped going because I got so busy involved with community affairs and other things, and I didn't really feel the desperate need for that kind of help. And if

I did, I thought I would just get it on my own, but if it really got bad, I'd go back to Al-Anon.

Mental Health

When lesbians, including many of the women in this study, turned to the medical community for help in combating feelings of shame, guilt, or confusion, the help they were given was questionable at best. During this period homosexuality was considered a psychological disorder, a form of mental illness that could be "cured." After being suspected or confirmed as lesbians, young women were often put into mental hospitals against their will and at their parents' urging. Convinced they were "sick," some women sought a "cure" of their own volition.

Carol, age seventy-four, spent many years in therapy trying to become heterosexual—without success. It was not until 1991, when she was in her late sixties, that she was fully able to admit to herself that she was lesbian and that changing her sexual orientation was not likely to happen.

I'd been trying for most of my adult life to change from being homosexual to getting cured, and I spent years and years and years in psychotherapy trying to do this because I was convinced that I was not really homosexual. I'd been told by a psychiatrist, when I was about twenty-five, a psychoanalyst, that I was not homosexual, that I just had a character defect that could be corrected. So I went into treatment with him and after about five years he said, "You've reached a plateau, and we just can't seem to go beyond this." So he turned me over to his wife, who was also a psychiatrist . . . and that lasted for about two sessions, I think. But through the years I've been in treatment with several other psychoanalysts and then with . . . a psychosynthesist, and he happened to be gay himself. And he allowed me to continue trying to get cured up until six years ago when he suddenly said to me, "You know, maybe you should consider the possibility that you really are lesbian." And it just never entered my mind that I would even consider such a thing because I'd been fighting against it for so many years. And about the same time I joined AA and this serenity prayer sort of spoke to me: "Grant me the serenity to accept the things I cannot change." And I thought, well, maybe I can't change this. So, then I kind a settled into the notion that, okay, maybe I really am homosexual.

Since it was not until 1973 that homosexuality was removed from the American Psychiatric Association's official manual of mental disorders, it is not surprising that the efforts of most of the mental health professionals up until then were directed toward "curing" gays and lesbians. This view persisted in the minds of many mental health professionals long after its removal from the list of mental illnesses. Other mental health professionals reassured women that they weren't really lesbian if they didn't act on their same-sex attractions. Helping people to recognize and affirm their homosexuality was not accepted practice until much more recently. The tools used most often to "cure" homosexuals were Freudian and other forms of talking analysis, which typically went on for years. Other methods from earlier eras included insulin shock, which was quite commonly used to combat lesbianism in female adolescents, and electroconvulsive shock therapy (ECT) for those who did not respond to other approaches. There are even cases where Dr. Walter Freeman's ice pick, the tool that produced the ultimate cure—the lobotomy—was used to treat recalcitrant homosexuals.

During the 1940s, Betty, now sixty-five, thought of herself as mentally deranged and a terrible person because she was lesbian. These kinds of thoughts were, of course, not atypical for lesbians of that period. Despite her distress, Betty did continue having relationships with women, including some married women. However, she was not happy and she turned to a psychiatrist for help.

> I finally ended up going to a psychiatrist and he tried to cure me. It was very unsatisfactory. He said, "Why do you hate your father?" Well, that's sort of like, "When did you quit beating your wife?" You know. "And do you have all these sexual fantasies?" Well, my father was an alcoholic and I thought the last thing I'd want to do is think about sex with my father. I thought, you know, yeah, I want to cut off his penis. And I thought I just wanted him to stop drinking. What does this have to do with . . . talking about that anyway?

Betty was not "cured." She twice almost married because of pressure from another psychiatrist, as well as pressure from her church.

But over the years, as public perceptions of lesbianism began to change, Betty became more accepting of herself. It was not until she was forty that she acknowledged that she wanted to live with another woman. Change for Betty has been slow in coming. Partnered and now retired, she still is not entirely comfortable with being lesbian and using the word "lesbian" to identify herself. She prefers "gay." After all, as she says, she is from the time when "homosexual" and "lesbian" were used synonymously with "pervert" and "depraved."

Sixty-six-year-old Phyllis had experiences with psychiatrists that were particularly traumatic. She married right out of high school, then fell in love with a woman and divorced her husband after fifteen years. Toward the end of her marriage, she developed phobias. Now, she attributes the problems in her marriage and the phobias to not having come to terms with being gay. The phobias were such a problem that she underwent psychiatric care for six years. However, her phobias continued with increasing severity to the point that she was unable to do such simple tasks as cash her paycheck. During the 1960s, she was twice hospitalized and subjected to electroconvulsive shock therapy. Fortunately, Phyllis eventually recognized that damage was being done to her and discovered that her cure lay in accepting her sexual orientation, not fighting against it.

> All this time the psychiatrist knew that I was attracted to women. I'd had truth serum numerous times and just blabbed. Well, he thought (I'd found out after I finally came out), he thought I was too nice of a person to be gay, and he thought that I would have a very unhappy life, and so he very much wanted to change me. That was the treatment. Well, I met my first partner in a mental hospital while I was there to be cured and after having some electroshock treatments, it makes you quite outgoing. So anyway, we were roommates, actually. You know, it was two years later that we actually got together, and we were together two years. My psychiatrist knew her also and said this is going to be a real disaster. He threatened to throw me out of therapy, and I said, "Well, I would quit. Yeah, I said I would quit going to him. I mean who was going to fire who here? Because I said for the first time in my life I know who I am, and my phobias immediately ceased. They were unrelenting except for maybe two, three weeks after electroshock, while you're still—your memory is—right, your brain's been fried. I didn't have any inhibi-

tions. And then I didn't worry about anything. And the second time they gave me a treatment, about a year following the first time, they brain-damaged me. And I ended up with damage for thirty days, simply to recover—my memory was so badly damaged, I could hardly find my way home from work. And I went back to work because, of course, I didn't remember that they told me not to. And finally it became so difficult for me to function, I finally called my psychiatrist and I said, "You know, I just can't continue this way," and so he sent me down and they put me on an unlocked ward simply to recover. . . . [I met this woman] in the institution. . . . She introduced me to other gay people, and my psychiatrist was right. It was not the relationship of the world, but I'll thank her for the rest of my life for bringing me out. And the day I came out, that I knew I was gay, my phobias stopped altogether. It was like being reborn. I could go to theaters, I could go out to eat, I could go to the bank, I could go to the grocery store and stand in line.

Medical Problems

Considering their ages, the number of participants who had severe medical problems was surprisingly quite limited. When asked about their health, most rated it as excellent or good. Those who did have health difficulties, however, found that other issues, such as ageism, homophobia, or self-image problems, often affected their treatment and recovery. It did not matter if the problem was a devastating diagnosis of cancer or a doctor's attitude; the women had to take charge and be responsible for their treatment even if it meant going beyond the usual medical practices.

Frances taught school for twenty years before moving to the West Coast and accepting a government position working with developmentally disabled people. She was diagnosed with breast cancer—twice. The psychological and physical effects of a double mastectomy were hard for her to overcome. When asked what were the hardest times in her life, she responded without hesitation.

Breast cancer. First and second time. The first time was really the hardest. The second time, not so bad. Probably the hardest time, and I'm being honest with you, would be [when] I had both breasts removed, so it would be your body image, you know? Coping with that and not seeing yourself as very attractive for a long time. I think that's the hardest. Mostly I decided that after the . . . especially after the second time that I'd find something good in every day and I've tried to do that. Something positive . . . and losing—I have a very close family. The hard part with the family is that they are fundamentalist Christians and they don't recognize me. . . . There weren't any [community support groups]. It was in 1984, and the only support group there was the American Cancer Society. It came and gave me something to put in my bra. I mean, there weren't any support groups as far as talking. Now there are; there are support groups for gay women. I'd love to have had a support group. It would have been wonderful because I was really frightened. . . . It was awful. It was really bad not having a support group. . . . And especially when you just found out. They're putting you through all these tests and checking your lungs out and all this stuff. And of course I was a smoker. That scared me even worse.

Frances felt, however, that in the end she would need to rely on herself. Although she acknowledges that her sister was there for her, she believes strongly that her inner strength pulled her through.

Jane, age fifty-nine, was diagnosed with breast cancer in 1987, and in 1994 developed ovarian cancer. Taking an active part in her disease is very important to her, and she believes that being an active participant is what has kept her alive this long.

Well, I've really taken an active part in my disease, which a lot of people don't do. I don't wait for the doctors to tell me; I tell them. I am a nurse so I do have a little bit of background but it is really not [in oncology]. I was an operating room nurse, so what do I know about cancer? But I try to understand what's going on. I don't let people do things to me that I don't understand. . . . I do what I need to do and I'm sure a lot of people get really angry about a nurse being so aggressive and that sort of thing, but it is my life. The reality is, I've got advanced cancer. It's going to kill me any minute. I'm bald. I really feel ugly. My cheeks are fat and I've got ascites in my abdomen and I can't do things—and hey, when is my next good day? I'm out of here. You know, you've only got one good chance, so why waste it? This is it. No one's coming. These are things I've learned the hard way. And, hey, let's go have a party.

Helen is seventy-three years old and has survived her cancer. Her life partner, who she met in 1945 in the military, died in 1995. After her own diagnosis of oral cancer and the death of her partner from lung cancer, Helen went into a severe depression. It was then that Helen became, as she said, "an activist," and it was her community involvement and activism that helped her through this traumatic time.

I had oral cancer in 1992, February of 1992. This month is my fifth year of survival. All my top teeth were taken out; my jawbone was taken out. I was on a feeding tube for two months and then it was a period of rehabilitation because I had to learn to talk all over again with a partially paralyzed tongue. And learn how to swallow because I had lost—again because of the partial paralysis and the lack of use—I had to learn how to swallow all over again. And that took nearly a year for recovery, and I think that was the worst because it was so hard, not on me so much, but on my partner because she had to eat all her meals alone and she hated that. And then the next bad part was she was diagnosed with lung cancer and the worst, the very worst part, was that we were told she only had three months to live. And watching her gradually disintegrate after being my life partner was very difficult. . . . The one thing we did do was lie and indicate that we were sisters . . . because if we didn't we neither could direct the medical care according to what we had discussed [or] to what we wanted. For example, when she learned she was terminal, she said, "Whatever you do, don't let them put me on any kind of machines. Just let me die. . . . Let me die with dignity. But I wouldn't have been able to do that unless I was indicated as a blood relative. For example, when she was in intensive care, I would not have been able to go in and see her and talk to her had I not been listed as her sister. . . . You stay out there on the outside looking in unless you tell a lie to get in. I think that should be changed. And I'm certainly fighting for [gay marriage] every instance that I get.

Eileen, age sixty-eight, is a retired nurse and well aware of what can happen in hospitals. She and her partner have taken all the legal steps they can to protect their rights. But her experience with a former partner does not totally assure her.

> Yeah, we've got a really good lesbian lawyer . . . We wanted a will, we wanted power of attorney, we wanted everything included in this thing that would eliminate any possibility that if one of us should become ill and have to go to the hospital, the other wouldn't have a problem with this visiting thing. We wanted to get that straight. I didn't have any trouble with [my former partner]. She had to have surgery and she said, "I'm not going [to surgery] unless Eileen can come and be in my room with me." And we had come out to the doctor. He said, "Oh yes, she can do that, if you want her in there." And she was going to the [hospital], so he got it all set up. I was to go there, be there right with her. Well, being a nurse, they should have been really happy I was going to be there. So I was in that room when she came back from surgery and some head nurse came and just raised hell because I was there. "You can't be here" —and went on and on and on. So I went home. [After] about a day this nurse calls, "Please come back." You know. And I finally did, and the doctor called too. . . . So I came back and I stayed in that room for six weeks. I gave her baths, I changed her linen—they should've been so happy to have me there. . . . I ate there; I even paid for those meals—and the food was lousy. But I don't want to go through that stuff again even though it did turn out all right. It was awfully traumatic for [my former partner], who was just out of surgery trying to make it. So we've gotten those things straight—we think; we don't know. We read and hear that [it] doesn't mean anything, the stuff in your will and in your power of attorney and all that. We're not afraid of our relatives getting in there and doing anything. What we're really hoping, seeing I'm a nurse, is that we can have our little intensive care right here and not have to go to a hospital.

Eileen and her partner took legal precautions they hope will ensure that their wishes will be recognized by a hospital when the time comes. For Claudia, age seventy-four, the time has arrived.

> I'm facing maybe some serious surgery. I'm just suffering from spinal stenosis. I don't know [if] you've ever heard of it; I

hadn't. I thought I was fairly well educated, although medical wise no one ever heard of that, and I turned up with it, and my God, what is it? Well, it's a narrowing of the spine. Yeah, down the base of the spine where the nerves all come out to the legs and the feet and the hips, clear down, and I'm having that, which is getting worse. I have a weakening, a lot of pain in my legs and feet. . . . Well, I finally got a diagnosis, which is half the battle because I go from—I had a doctor, an internist, a man. . . . When I fired him, some good things happened because his nurse said, "My God, what's the matter?" I said, "I just feel like he doesn't hear me and he sent me here and there." And I said, "There's something wrong and I'm not getting anywhere." So she said, "I'll call the visiting nurse." . . . This physical therapist came and said to me—I'm sure he was a gay young man, seemed to be—he said to me, "What's your diagnosis?" And I said, "I don't have one. I've been trying to find out what my problem is." He said, "Go see a neurologist." . . . I found a neurologist and I found a woman [who made the diagnosis]. I'm having to go to [a large city] to the university hospital because if I'm going to have surgery, I want someone that really knows what they're doing. . . . If I have to have something like that done . . . I want to have the best. And I want to have confidence in them; I don't want somebody that scares me. Yes, I'm scared to have this operation. . . . I'm hoping that everything will . . . that I'll get so I can do things.

Claudia faced discrimination and she had to overcome ageism, sexism, and homophobia within the medical professions just to be taken seriously—a situation that could endanger her health. Fortunately, she has been persistent. Having spent most of her life being an advocate for others, Claudia decided that she needed to advocate for herself.

I think they say, "Oh well, you're seventy-four, what the heck." . . . I think they just think, well, you're an old woman so why? We're not going to repair you or fix you up. You don't have much time left anyway. I really feel that's—and the males are generally, sort of have that attitude toward women. I guess if I were an old man I might be treated differently. Maybe not, because it is an ageist thing.

Homophobia also may have played a role in Claudia's experience. Her partner, who is somewhat butch in appearance, took Claudia in to see the doctor and went into the examining room with her. The doctor seemed uncomfortable and Claudia experienced a negative reaction.

> I think it may have bothered him because I did notice after that his attitude sort of changed toward me. But I thought, oh, maybe this is my . . . I'm not sure. Looking back on it, I'm pretty sure there was some discrimination.

Currently, Claudia needs surgery to relieve the constant and debilitating pain, but she finds now that most doctors are reluctant to perform surgery and suspects it is because of her age and gender. She continues her search for a responsive doctor.

Chapter 7

Resiliency

I think of all the hazards I've been through—have only made me stronger.

Ernestine, age seventy-five

The majority of the women featured in this book recognized their lesbianism at a time when society, in general, obdurately practiced what John Stuart Mill referred to as "social tyranny" and the "tyranny of the prevailing opinion" to enforce heterosexuality, rigid gender definitions, and acceptable roles and behavior (Castell, 1947, p. 4). In the early 1960s the stultifying repression of the 1930s through the 1950s started to crack, finally giving way to sweeping cultural changes brought about by the civil rights movement, gay liberation, Beatlemania, flower power, drugs, the Vietnam War, and the women's movement.

With the cultural change came spreading sexual experimentation and a fluidity of gender roles. Many lesbians, especially younger women, refused to remain invisible and moved out into the open with pride. The lesbians interviewed for this book, being older and having faced oppression in ways their younger counterparts never experienced, were slower, in general, in coming out, in claiming gay pride, and in finding and organizing community groups.

Yet, whatever the adversity they faced, these women took control of their lives, albeit some sooner than others. In this chapter, the women relate how they found their strength and support, and share their dreams for the future. For most of those interviewed, the liberation movements were not a primary influence on their evolving views of themselves or the status of lesbians in society. What was crucial, however, in allowing them to accept themselves and to live their lives was the direct, personal support from partners, friends, parents, children, and the larger gay and straight communities, including churches and twelve-step programs.

The importance of support in these women's lives cannot be over-emphasized. Without it, many of their individual successes would not have occurred. Many of the women also shared how they found strength from within. Some pointed to self-reliance as the key to their survival. Others credited their spirituality and the larger meaning in life. A few had lesbian mentors to ease the way, but most learned through individual trial and error. They are resilient survivors who have a sense of pride in who they are and what they accomplished. Their courage and tenacity cannot help but inspire our respect and admiration. They did what needed to be done to achieve their goals and they look back with very few regrets. Their lives represent amazing resiliency.

I KNOW WHO I AM

In spite of growing up in a society that insisted on homosexual strictures and invisibility, most of the women now have a clear sense of who they are—and are pleased about it. Self-acceptance, a strong sense of self, and enduring fortitude all provided these women with important tools for overcoming the adversity in their lives. As might be expected, the acquisition of a confident sense of self was gained or maintained with varying degrees of ease or difficulty. For some it continues to be a work in progress.

Christine, age sixty-four, married as she was expected to do and stayed married for ten years for the sake of the children despite her realization that she was attracted to women. She did have relationships with a couple of women during her marriage but felt tremendously guilty at the time. As she has matured, she grew to appreciate the importance of self-acceptance as providing a solid foundation for her own strength.

> But I feel I was born a lesbian—oh yeah, as I look back, I was always different. I was always just a step to the right or a step to the left, I could never—it was as if I just moved a little to the right or left, you know? I was just always kind of outside looking in or poltergeist, you know, looking down on this life that

was supposed to include me but didn't. I didn't really feel accepted until I absolutely accepted myself.

Jill's experience was much like Christine's in that she followed societal expectations of the 1950s by marrying and having children. Eventually she got divorced and now, in her fifties, is coming to terms with being a lesbian. She shared the importance of believing in herself and an enduring sense that she can make it through the most difficult of times.

> I'm just kind of figuring out who I am. . . . I'm just now identifying all that repression, not being able to be an individual, trying to fit into what they wanted me to be . . . I'm just discovering me. . . . Each time I come through a transition or a time of knowing, I feel this is great. And it really keeps getting better. It's fighting sometimes and it's struggling sometimes and sometimes I just—I'll start feeling like, "Oh God, I don't know if I'll make it." But that happens less and less. Now I always know I'm going to make it! This hurts sometimes; I don't understand what's going on, why I am feeling this way—but now I know I can make it. When I was younger, I always—I didn't know.

Frances, now fifty-nine, learned about the importance of inner strength when she was much, much younger. She had married a gay man and moved with him to California. Shortly after arriving in California she was in a serious car accident and was unable to get around by herself. Her husband was gone much of the time looking for an apartment, working, and so forth. She was left alone. Frances, like several others, emphasized the role of self-reliance in facing whatever came her way.

> [Where] I gained my strength was I used to cry every night, for nights and nights and nights because I was in this cast and I couldn't do anything; I couldn't go anywhere. I felt really sorry for myself. It was the best experience that ever happened to me. Having to be alone and not having anybody to rely on, I started to rely on myself. . . . I feel that I have a lot of inner strength and I don't need a lot of support. But I do need [some] support and I get it when I need it. I think you also get support by being able to give it. I think I am able to do that. I really feel very comfortable.

Throughout her life, Elaine, age fifty-seven, experienced and overcame a number of disappointments and potentially damaging emotional traumas. At this point she likes herself and her life and shares her ability to carry on despite the hurdles she may face.

> I'm real happy with the way I've been able to do some real inner stuff when I look back to where I was when I was eighteen and where I am now. Of course that is maturation too. But the scared little kid at that point and the path I've been able to take through losing friends and changing careers and not having the career I thought I wanted which were real painful parts of my life. I look back and think, "well you got through it," and I like where I've been. And I'm looking forward to where I'm going.

At seventy-five years of age, Ernestine describes herself as undaunted by tragedy, resourceful, and in charge. She also reflects on how the adversity in her life has provided her with courage and a deep appreciation for life and the unfolding of each day.

> So I think all of the hazards I've been through have only made me stronger. . . . I think the most important thing is integrity, honesty, the desire—I'm not a do-gooder; I just want—I'm free as a flower to blossom, and I don't want to be encumbered. . . . I want the ability to have a clear thought in my mind every morning I wake up and I look for the unfolding of the new day and what the day means to my life, and those whom my life touches.

SOURCES OF SUPPORT

Many women shared how their strength and resilience was garnered from multiple sources, such as parents, partners, friends, and their own determined efforts. All of these women have a strong sense of self, independence, and an ability to carry on, but if they did not have support, whether from partner, family, friend, or self, they probably would not have overcome the pressures of society. Fortunately, these women did have support from those around them that, to one degree or another, enabled them to live their lives and handle the stresses and obstacles they faced. Early parental support, which encouraged "can do" attributes such as a belief in oneself and the ability to try anything, clearly helped these women accept themselves and reach their personal goals. Many initially relied on their parents, grandparents, and siblings, and later came to rely on their chosen families—of partners, children, and friends as well as biological family—for love, encouragement, acceptance, and support.

Raised in a rural eastern state by her mother (her father having died when she was very young), Judy, now fifty-seven, considered her childhood "absolutely dreadful." Isolated, poor, disliked by classmates because she was too smart, she learned fast that she would have to get an education on her own. In spite of her father's wishes that both she and her brother go to college, only her brother received help from people in the community after her father's death. Nonetheless, drawing upon her mother's example and with the help of one of her professors at the small college she was attending, she was able to transfer to one of the Seven Sister colleges and become a college graduate.

> I was raised by a single mother who was a very proud, very bright, very capable woman, and I think I learned from her that you really have to take care of yourself and have confidence in yourself. I didn't develop that when I was a kid; it took me a long time. I mean after all, I'm fifty-seven; I was a teenager during the 1950s. I've been through all the years of oppression. I've been through all the years of a society telling me that women don't know anything and women can't do anything and all those kind of things. There's been a lot of that crap and it causes tremendous insecurity and uncertainty and hesitation and all that, but under it I think I kept putting one foot in front of another because my mother had managed to give me an example of putting one foot ahead of another, even when things were really, really bad.

In 1966 Judy went on to Stanford Law School, a decision that suited her well and led to many accomplishments. She is the first to recognize that she was able to surmount the overwhelming poverty, isolation, and educational mediocrity of her youth to become who she is today because of the support from her mother and her partner, as well as her own determined efforts.

Some of it is certainly from [my partner]. And I say a lot of it is from within. . . . . And [support] from other people I've met along the way and from rewards that I've gotten along the way, academic rewards and things of that kind that have reinforced the idea that I am capable.

Charlotte was born in 1923 and grew up on a farm in rural Washington State. She graduated from high school shortly after World War II, and entered and graduated from university. Later she became very active in union organizing. She described the support she received as a combination of financial and moral support from her family, and strength and support from friends. She also suggested that her own choices played a role in her life's accomplishments.

I never asked my family for much. Well, we came from an era of time that you went out of the nest and got a job, and my parents did help me to go to school. And that was a struggle because, hey, my dad was a blue-collar worker and we're talking— I started at the university in 1948, and when I got out of the university it [was] 1952, 1953. Jobs were tough then. . . . I would say the family gave me the support of, you know, I guess moral support, and friends did too. . . . I've had some really good breaks, but maybe I've made some for myself.

For a few women, parental support included an acceptance of their sexual orientation. Looking back from her perspective of seventy-one years, Ann said that she is fortunate to consider her relationship with her family a "great thing." From early on, she felt the love and support of her parents. Her father, a firm believer in education, encouraged her to attend a young women's academy, which she did. She prospered academically, and in an all-women setting she gained self-confidence and went on to do well at university. Ann's parents believed in education for its own sake—not simply as a means to meet someone to marry. They knew Ann was lesbian and never pressured her to marry.

My mother was the great strength in my life when I was young. She was just a marvelous woman. Also my father. Of course, you know, they were both just wonderful and . . . my mother was a very strong woman, a very loving woman, although she never was a hugger like my dad. . . . So they balanced each other. . . . I remember one time when I was living with [a former partner], one of her sisters, my aunt, got really upset with my lifestyle and wrote me this really scathing letter; she told my mother that she should disown me. And my mother told her to butt out. And I think it was unfortunate that their relationship for years was really nil. . . . My mother was very strong. . . . She would criticize me at times, but never about my relationship. . . . If anyone else criticized me, my mother was like a banshee. So she was really a strong influence in my life, to recognize that there are strong women and she was a very strong woman.

A few women explained that other biological family members, such as grandparents and siblings, were very supportive. Elaine, age fifty-seven when she was interviewed, was raised in a small, close-knit rural community on the West Coast. Because she knew of no other gays and lesbians, she felt very isolated and detached from her community. She found no support within the confines of the small-town morality of the period. Like the majority of the lesbians interviewed, Elaine feared the stigma of being labeled a lesbian. She thought she could resolve her problem by working abroad as a civilian with the military.

I thought if I go to Europe and if I'm around a great many men working with the military—there weren't as many women involved at that point—that I would meet somebody and all this would go away. I would settle down, get married, have the 2.5 kids, and live happily ever after. And so that's what I was hoping for. . . . [I was] really trying very hard to be just like everybody else and not feeling so alone a lot of the time. It didn't work.

When Elaine returned to the United States in the early 1970s, she found that the public perception of homosexuals was starting to change, and activists were shoving open the closet door. She was overwhelmed and she "couldn't believe that people were out, that there were women's bars." It was in those bars that Elaine discovered that, as she put it, "I finally belonged somewhere, and with a group of people that were real supportive and I could finally kind of unfold."

Back in the United States in a different climate, Elaine was able to accept being a lesbian and eventually come out to different members of her family. Her grandmother's support was particularly important.

> We have our ups and downs like any other group of people that are related; we're all very Germanic, and I'm very proud of that identity. We get very stubborn and everybody kind of digs in their hind legs and we just kind of fold our arms and that's it. But we're there for each other; we care about each other. And it's a group of people that are very supportive of me. . . . My German grandmother was my favorite person in the entire world when I came out. I asked Mother, "Do I tell Grandma?" She was in her eighties then. She said, "Well, I don't know. I don't know that Grandma is going to understand." Grandma came over to visit, years ago, and I was in my apartment, and I was doing something. And I looked over, and she was sitting there reading [the gay newspaper]—and I thought, oh, boy! She didn't say anything, but like an hour or so later, she said, "Elaine?" I said, "Yes, Grandma." And she said, "You're never going to get married, are you?" I said, "No, Grandma." She said, "Hmmm, I didn't think so. But that's okay. Whatever you are, I love you." And the subject never came up again. So that to me is what family is. Close.

With a growing sense and acceptance of her own identity, combined with newfound support, Elaine was able to focus on her goals and help build a sense of community. She pursued a job as a counselor and then as a director of a newly formed gay and lesbian counseling service. Elaine found that the sexual minority community supported her efforts to start a counseling service and the various pieces, including funding, fell into place.

> When I was the [director] at the [nonprofit counseling service] . . . we lost our funding at one point. Not because of the gay agency, but because we were clinically not doing a very good job. I was able to hire some good staff and turn that around, and we became recognized in 1979 as one of the best agencies in the county. . . . I made some inroads into the county board of mental health, got on the mayor's task force, the police task force . . . and it opened a lot of doors. I ran into a lot of real supportive

people and it really helped me to sort of get real clear about who I was, where I wanted to go, how I wanted to get there, as much as one ever knows. But it really added to my strength and my feeling good about who I was as a lesbian.

Partners provided pivotal support to the women interviewed, be it emotional, financial, or simply a steady presence. Ann's current partner is now the mainstay of her life. She and Helen, a retired nurse, have been together for over eleven years. "And now in my life my greatest strength is in Helen. Helen has given me strength in so many ways . . . showing me she truly loves me and wants to spend her life with me. . . . She is always a continuing inspiration."

Denise, at age fifty-seven, is one of the younger lesbians interviewed. She explained that her parents knew early on that she was a lesbian and accepted it: "They had always accepted my partner as my partner." The most important source of support in her life comes from her current partner.

> I get an awful large percentage of [support] through my relationship with [my partner], and have for the last quarter of a century. So I'd say that certainly is number one. . . . It feels as though if I didn't have her, it wouldn't be enough!

A number of the women who were not currently in a primary relationship addressed the question of feeling good about themselves without having to be partnered to do so. Ruth is fifty-eight and has lived alone for the last twenty-seven years, most recently for seventeen years in the same apartment.

> What I want is a relationship with someone who's happy in her own home and we can see each other when it's convenient. . . . I'm pretty well content with being alone with my cat. I cannot see myself living day in day out with another person. . . . I was talking with one of the lesbians at work the other day. She said that most people are in couples; that's the way the world goes, but every once in a while you come across a person who is a couple within themselves. Who is one within themselves. I say that sounds like me.

Janet, also age fifty-eight, lives alone and has done so for a number of years. Previously she had an on-again, off-again relationship with a married woman. When that ended she started drinking heavily and eventually sought help through AA. Now she is happy with herself, her job, and with living alone.

> You know, I have friends who one day they're with this one three months, six months it was the last one. I can't understand it. Of, course I don't know if that's the way they are, but I just couldn't be like that. I mean, I am happy alone, and people say, "Well how could you be happy by yourself?" Well, I love me.

Many of the women interviewed spoke of how friends were indispensable in providing needed support. Often a friend, or friends, assumed a critical supportive role by providing help such as a place to stay, help in finding a job, or, most important, emotional support.

Seventy-one-year-old Kay is a self-confident and self-assured woman. As a result of the death of her mother in childbirth, a paternal aunt and uncle raised Kay. She joined the military, attended a university, married several times, and was divorced for the last time in 1949. After earning her PhD, Kay entered private practice in the field of mental health and over time earned recognition as an expert witness in the judicial system. She was not, however, out. She lived a closeted lesbian life until she and her partner retired. She then made up for lost time by becoming a moving force within the lesbian community.

Kay did not experience the stresses of poverty or the lack of support; she grew up surrounded by family and friends who encouraged her to be in control of her life. While acknowledging her own self-efficacy, Kay found her family and friends to be important sources of support.

> I had parents who gave me a very good basis for self-confidence. I could do what I've wanted to do and I've done it. I feel very powerful, as far as I am in charge of my life—I've always been. I don't feel that anybody can harm me, really. And this is how I have been for a good many years and I still am. . . . I've had strength and support from friends. I have some very good friends, very close friends, longtime friends, and some new friends that are very important to me.

Such recognition of the support received from family and friends, however, did not lessen Kay's sense that she is responsible for her life and is, when all is said and done, the source of her own strength. When asked where she found her strength and support she replied, "Within myself I've found it."

Twenty-two years younger than Kay, Sharon, age fifty-nine, also acknowledged the importance of friends and family in building self-confidence and strength and the recognition that true support often comes from within.

> I think my grandfather and my father to some degree gave me great inner strength. I always felt like I could handle any problem. Always have tried to be supportive of other people. So I think part of it is inner strength, and the other is usually from a close relationship, if I have one. The times in my life when I haven't had one . . . I rely on my friends . . . and they've always been there for me.

Similar to some of the other women interviewed, Catherine described the importance of her own children as a source of support. Now sixty-three, Catherine explained that she knew at an early age that she did not want to marry and become a traditional housewife. Yet, she married because of social pressures and raised five children. Eventually she realized that she was physically and emotionally attracted to women. After hearing Sonia Johnson speak about her break with the Mormon Church, Catherine realized that she wanted to go to school and pursue her own goals. She divorced her husband, accepted that she was a lesbian, and proceeded to live her life.

> And like I do everything, I told my kids. Not right away. It was a while later and I did one at a time. And they were okay with it. I mean they weren't shocked. . . . I guess they're kind of used to my doing different things, because I told them different things as they got older and I got more able to talk to them about certain things. I had shared with them a lot of things about my life. And they've just been really supportive.

Catherine has not had a long-term relationship with a woman, but has always had a large, strong support system including a number of gay men. Now she finds that her main source of support is from her chosen family.

> I find strength and support from my family—to a certain extent. I would say my sister, my women friends, very definitely. I would say very definitely Inez, the woman that has lung cancer—if she doesn't make it, it's going to be very, very difficult. She's been my support for the past seven years. We've supported each other. . . . As I get older I realize that loss is going to be a part of getting older. I also have, like I say, a couple of— particularly Warren, who is a gay man, we've been very close. . . . My kids, but they've got their own lives. It's a different kind of support. They've got their own stuff going on. . . . I want to have my own peers.

At the age of sixty-nine, Pat found that her support network changed dramatically when she faced the death of her partner. Early in life, Pat responded to the social pressures of her time by marrying, having children, and living a straight life. After twenty-four years of marriage, she divorced, recognized her sexuality, and moved with her lesbian partner to a small rural arts community. After her partner died, Pat considered moving to a different area but decided against another move. As a single, bereaved lesbian, she found that lesbian couples were not always welcoming. She feels estranged from the "gay community" and now receives the majority of her support from older straight women who share many of her life experiences, including the death of a partner.

> I don't feel like I have a gay family. I lost Katy; I lost a lot of people. . . . And the community in general here—and I don't mean to bad-mouth them, they're all good people—they do the couple thing. The couples have their cliques . . . and they just don't think about inviting the [single] people. . . . So I'm in a lonely stage although I have a lot of straight friends. . . . And believe it or not, straight women have been my support. They all know I'm gay; I can talk about it—a few of them it took a while. Had to kind of just be patient. Sooner or later they deal with it. And it's been a major support. These are wonderful women. They're from every walk of life, education-wise, money-wise; they're all older. We've all gone through life and we have a lot to

talk about. The group has been in existence for five and a half years. So I lived for that weekly meeting for a long time after Katy went. So it's been straight women that have really supported me.

Sylvia, age sixty-seven, a nurse, educator, and recently retired, chose to live away from other gays and lesbians in general and the gay and lesbian community in particular. Sylvia shares some things in common with Pat. She married twice, divorced twice, and raised four children. Unlike Pat, all the while she had a number of closeted lesbian liaisons until twenty-six years ago when she met her current partner, Rachel. Sylvia is active in her city's community affairs and believes "there isn't any way I could ever be [out]." As a result Sylvia and Rachel are as separated from other lesbians as Pat is. Sylvia emphasized the importance of her relationship and characterized her support as being

> From within. Nobody else . . . there isn't anything [a gay support group]. I think there is further down on the coast but it isn't something we—Rachel is still working. I'm retired but I'm quite involved in city politics so I don't think it would behoove either one of us to get involved very much. It doesn't help the situation. No I don't want that. I don't need support anyway. We're fine.

For other women interviewed, the concept of community was an important factor in surviving in a society that preferred they remain invisible. For some of the women, especially those over sixty-five, events such as the gay liberation movement following the events at the Stonewall Inn, even though they did not participate directly, provided them with a connection to the broader community. This helped some make a transition from a closeted way of life to a more open and out way of life. They could now join lesbian discussion groups, activity groups, and various other social and political groups to whatever extent they desired. For others, community provided a sense of security and energy. They no longer needed to stand alone.

Growing up during the Depression, Eleanor, age seventy-two, was extremely cognizant of the importance of maintaining a livelihood. She described herself as a "survivor," and said her survival has been made easier by the support she receives from her community.

Certainly, my older sister. And friends. Other lesbians and some gay men, too. Certainly in community. I couldn't have survived without the [gay and lesbian community]. It's my vitamins. I work with straight people all the time, but I can't survive there. I need this contact, this relationship . . . I feel a real need to always be in contact with lesbians. Helps my soul.

BEST TIMES

The capacity to adapt to change and the perseverance shown by the women interviewed for this book stems from a number of sources. In addition to the support they received from others, positive life experiences also contributed. One approach to understanding how they became resilient was to ask them about the best times in their lives, anticipating that these positive experiences helped build their skills, their competence, and confidence as well as helped to offset the worst times. Not surprisingly, the women identified a wide variety of experiences when they spoke about the best times. They talked about their school and college experiences, their careers, their adolescent crushes and adult romantic relationships, their accomplishments, and their journeys to being and accepting themselves. For a great many of the women the best times were now. Getting older has meant that they are freer to be themselves and do what they want to do.

Laura, age fifty-seven, grew up in a hardworking family that stressed education as a means of bettering oneself. She knew that when she was eighteen she would be expected to take on adult responsibilities but in the meantime she could enjoy her childhood.

> The best times in my life were the times I spent at school, and this was elementary, junior high, and high school. I truly didn't have any worries when I was going to school. I didn't have to hurry up and be and adult. I didn't have to assume adult responsibilities. My parents truly allowed us to be children. . . . I truly didn't have to worry about anything, so that for me was one of the best times of my life.

Maria's sisters recognized her lesbianism and supported her when she came out at age thirteen. They encouraged her to work hard, go to college, and they trusted her to succeed in whatever she wanted to do.

Now sixty-three, she recalls her college days as especially memorable.

> I would say the best time of my life, a period in which I was very optimistic and gaining in self-confidence in my own ability to do things, was with my first love. I started college then and the intellectual part of me was nurtured and grew. Those were probably the best years.

Frances, age fifty-nine, looked back and concluded that the best time of her life was when she found the courage to stand up to societal and family pressure to marry.

> Well, I think probably the best time—one of the best times in my life was when I decided who I would be. I was engaged to be married, because that's what you did in those days; you got married. All my friends got married and I became engaged. I think one of the most remarkable times in my life is when I decided that I didn't want to be married, that I wanted to be a lesbian. I was twenty-one years old. I said to myself, you have a choice in your life. Either you can get married and do what everybody thinks you should, or do what you want to do. So what do you want to do? How would you be the happiest? And I decided I'd be happiest not married.

Without a doubt, Susan's estrangement from her family following her divorce brought home to her the importance of connections with friends and community. Now fifty-six, she identified community involvement as her best time.

> For me the good old days were the early days of the women's movement. Those were the days I'd go back to when I reminisce. Those are the memories that make me feel that my life has been worthwhile and I participated in making changes.

Relationships, and especially long-term partnerships, were heavily represented in the "best times" category. Eleanor, age seventy-two, is surprised to be with a woman much younger than herself.

Well, probably the best time in my life is right now. Absolutely. It's crazy, but it is. I can't remember ever being this happy or content. I like—I'm a good partner and I like partnership so the happiest times in my life have always been when the partnership has been good.

Denise, fifty-seven, also found that now she and her partner were experiencing the best time of their lives in spite of her partner retiring early due to medical problems. "Well, I think the best time of my life is right now, really. . . . I'll tell you these early retirement years for us have been wonderful, so this is just the best time of my life."

These sentiments were echoed by Barbara, age sixty-nine, about her life with her partner of eighteen years.

[M]y current partner who's—it's a loving, comfortable relationship that allows me to be myself. . . . For a long time now—ever since the beginning—it's been getting better with age and certainly with retirement we can do the things that we love to do together. We can travel and we can appreciate each other in our lives. And each day is a wonderful new beginning.

Muriel, fifty-eight years of age, married, had children, and divorced after meeting her current partner twenty-five years ago.

[I] can't say that the thirteen and a half years that I was married were so bad; certainly had some good times and I've always enjoyed our children. I think though, without question, I've never been as happy as I am now and my life has been kind of emotional . . . I cannot imagine not having her [partner], and I think the other thing [is] things just seem so much more comfortable. I think that the older I get the more comfortable [I get]. Probably it's my own self confidence.

SPIRITUALITY

Many credited the spiritual aspects of their lives with providing the strength they need to face the challenges they encountered and to bounce back from misfortune. A deep sense of or belief in spirituality or a personal philosophy provided many of the women with purpose and meaning. Mary, age fifty-five, depends on the money she earns from her writings, which as she says, "is not much." But she is happy and planning for the future. Her spirituality brings her peace and she credits it with enabling her to do as she likes. It is where she turns first for answers.

> In my Native American spirituality practices, that's the first place that I always go whether I go to a sweat or I go to a pow-wow or I go beat my drums or I smoke my pipe, sit and talk to my creator. Whatever I do, that's the first resource for me. The second resource is inside of me. . . . . And then if I still need more, then I will call friends, call a therapist, and get support from other people. But the first place is my own spiritual practices and I do that on a daily basis. The Creator and I are tuned in. I mean it's really a strong thing for me.

When Ernestine, age seventy-five, was in New York, she met a woman who was a Christian Scientist. Because of the way the woman carried herself, her composure and her general conduct, she became a role model for Ernestine.

> I've been a student of Christian Science for over fifty years. It was just perfect for my attitude; that's the way I was all along. All I needed was a label to put on it. So that's been the greatest influence in my life. . . . There's only one power, and we're all praying to the same power regardless of what the label is. . . . No matter what the religion is, if it's Buddha, a whatever it is, we have the opportunity to recognize that when you have a problem that there is a solution and it's right there. If you just turn the page, you've eradicated it. . . . A friend of mine was having a problem. I said go get a pen, inflate a balloon and right before you inflate them, write down the problem—each problem. Take that fist of balloons. Take them out and just let them go. And just wait for the answer. Because you can't solve it. You've got to release and rely. . . . Every experience I have gives me a more solid foundation [of faith]. It's not because I have a false sense of stability or false sense of reliance. I know the power is there.

Barbara is a seventy-eight-year-old very private person. Her previous long-term partner was extremely closeted and this added to

Barbara's deep sense of privacy. Her current partner of eighteen years has been instrumental in providing a new and more open life. In addition to finding strength in her primary relationship, Barbara identified her twelve-step program as her spiritual path.

> I'm a recovering alcoholic and I find that [twelve-step program] as a way of life is a very healthy one and I find a lot of support and real substance in practicing that as a way of life. And the spirituality—as opposed to a church cathedral kind of—my spirituality and my cathedral is the out of doors. And my spirituality stems from trying to practice the kind of loving relationships with other people that I would like to have other people relate to me.

Nancy, age sixty-two, spoke of the spiritual beliefs that guide her life as determinist and unchangeable. Even when she referred to unpleasant and devastating events in her past, she did so without rancor.

> I believe that there is a master plan and I believe that everything that happens to you, no matter how bad you think it is at the time . . . that's what was meant to be. I believe that everything that happens to you is meant to be—exactly how it happens to you is part of whatever the master plan is for your life. I don't think you can change anything that is supposed to happen to you. If you're supposed to die today, you'll die today: win the lotto today, you'll win the lotto. . . . I still think that even the bad things that happened in my life that I thought were just devastating at the time, I know there's a reason for that. I guess I've always been willing to accept those things and I've never understood people who can't.

Eileen, age sixty-eight, reflected on her sources of strength over the years. Like many of the women, her focus has shifted from organized religion to a more personalized spiritual practice that for her, draws heavily on connections with others.

> I think when I was really young [strength and support] came from religion. My folks were very insistent that we go to Sunday school and church and Christian endeavor and all kinds of stuff. . . . I think I did get a lot of strength from that. Later I got a

lot of strength from my interest in nature and just being around the woods and the lake and stuff. I told you I'm a recovering alcoholic so I've gotten a lot of strength from AA. An awful lot. And I've been in it for a million years. I'm very interested in Indian spirituality—done a lot of reading. I get a lot of strength from the younger gays and lesbians because I think they've got a lot of strength, so I borrow some of it. They do a lot of things I would have liked to do when I was young. But I would say the basic thing is AA. We give each other a lot of strength; we help each other an awful lot.

DREAMS AND DESIRES

Even though many of the women described current times as the best of times, they still had dreams and desires yet to be fulfilled. Many spoke of looking forward to everyday pleasures such as a good meal, puttering in the garden, or sitting home at night with a cat on their lap. Some had plans to grow their retirement fund, travel, write, or learn a new skill. Others outlined their hopes for remedying the world's ills. Whatever the content, these dreams and visions reflected the women's experiences as well as their abiding values. These values reflect both their struggles and their resilience.

If she could, Pat, age sixty-nine, would change societal attitudes toward women and lesbians at the time she was born so that her life could have been easier.

If I was born today, I would be in a gay lifestyle early in my life. If I was to do it again, I sure wouldn't want to miss having had kids. See what I'm saying? But I'd try to be gay right from day one, if that's what I felt I was. I'd go for more education. It's my big regret not getting more education, but I had no support. Depression era, poor family, no one told me I could do it on my own. It was never said. I probably could have, but I didn't know it. More education. And lesbians have to have it. They know they're going to be supporting themselves their whole life. They're not going to have a husband, so they get more education. That's what I admire about the lesbians I've met. They really seem to educate themselves and they do well. They are professionals. That's what I'd do. Because I found out too late that I was smart.

Rhonda, age sixty, who felt compelled to cut short her military career, would like to change the negative military attitude and culture toward homosexuals.

> I would like our citizens to wake up—when your military's policy is that homosexuality is incompatible with the military, I would like you and everybody else to be angry enough to change that. That's dreadful for all those who are in, probably for women it's 15 percent. The numbers were very much higher when I was in. That is a lot of women.

Kay, seventy-one, and active in bettering life for older lesbians, when asked what things would she change if she could, replied:

> Well, I would change the limits on the life span. I'd like to live longer. Trying to do everything I want to do. . . . Well, I'm going to do it. I don't really have any regrets. Maybe I could have done more, but I did all I could and I'm happy with it. I've done the things I wanted to do. When I was in the [military] I wanted to be a pilot. Well that was out for women; that was totally impossible. But I always wanted to be a pilot. So when I could afford to I bought an airplane and started flying lessons . . . so I was a pilot. I enjoyed that for a number of years. [Then] I wanted a swimming pool. I looked at all the pools in town and got one with a house to go with it. And when I sold the airplane I bought an RV and drove around the country. I've been to Europe. . . . I've been everywhere I wanted to go, and I've done everything I've wanted to do, and I'm still doing it. There are a lot more things I'm going to do. But I can't say I regret not having done them sooner—then I'd have done them.

ADVICE FOR YOUNGER GENERATIONS

Many of the women expressed their appreciation for being asked to have their voices heard. Comments such as "Thank you for letting me participate" and "This is so exciting that I will get to contribute to my community" were common. As elders, these women had advice to share with younger lesbians. They offered their perspective on topics ranging from the aging process and how to prepare for it to self-confidence and how to live in society. When offering their advice, a number of the women stated that being true to oneself, being brave, and having self-confidence are paramount to successful living and aging.

The importance of friends and community was reflected in Mary's advice. At fifty-five, she is currently partnered, and living with a life-threatening illness. She has deep spiritual connections, and has been an activist in several movements. She urged younger women to care for themselves and for those around them.

> Take care of yourself. Especially as a woman, because I don't think society's going to do it. I think that you need to prepare yourself before you get old. I think this is a retrospective answer in some ways because obviously I didn't do enough of it. If I had the capacity now that I'm a little bit older to sock more away to take care of myself, I'd do it. But that's an important thing to do. Take care of yourself and to not always worry about your family, whether your family's not accepting you or not—just pick a family, pick a chosen family. Hold on to them. Hold on to those friendships. They take attendance—they take daily attendance— and I think you need to pay attention to that. I think a lot of young people don't know that. . . . And so, go ahead and pay attention to your needs and pay attention to the needs of your friends because I think that they're the most valuable family you're ever going to have. I know I've had a couple of friends say to me . . . "Probably when you get to be an old lady, you're going to have to live with us." But you know, it's something special to have somebody say that and to say, "I want to be there for you."

Many women also urged those coming after them to be true to themselves. These women's struggles with coming out, raising children, and planning for the future were all influenced by their ability to love themselves despite the obstacles.

At seventy-one, Edith reflected on the importance of accepting oneself.

Don't be afraid. You're entitled to be who you are. Make a real effort to get some help if things are going badly for you. I think that's good advice to anybody, whoever they are. Remember that there are a lot of other things that make you who you are besides being a capital "L" lesbian. Enjoy!

Given the turbulent times that many of the women in this study went through, it is not surprising that some of them offered self-knowledge and honesty with oneself as advice to younger women. For sixty-four-year-old Christine, a sense of self-truth is fundamental to each person's life journey. She urged other lesbians not to hide from their interest in women.

Know and love themselves. Know themselves. Truth is everything. Don't be afraid to be honest with yourself, even though it's painful. Gee, if you're not—if a gal even suspects she might be interested in women, explore it. For God's sake, don't run from it, because it's a wonderful experience. It's everything to me. I am what I am. I've had people ask me why I'm a lesbian, and all I could say is, "Why are you not? Why are you a heterosexual?" I can't answer that. Like the fellow in *Zorba the Greek* said, "My books tell me I can't answer questions like yours." Just be true to yourself. Don't follow anybody else's—that's something that's really important that I've observed. Follow that. Don't put yourself down.

Laura, age fifty-seven, echoed Christine's advice to be true to oneself. For her, that means finding strength from within and loving oneself.

They have to love themselves and they have to find strength in themselves and to be whatever it is that they want to be. If they happen to be a lesbian, they still will have to find ways to get around whatever barriers may be put in their way, whatever roadblocks may be put in their way. They have to be who they are. But they have to love themselves first. That's the universal wisdom I would give to anyone, any lesbian or anyone else— I would tell them to love themselves and to thine own self be true.

Charlotte, age sixty-seven, took the advice to be true to oneself one step further: She suggested using a strong sense of self to change things for the better. "Advice—don't let the bastards get you down. I think, be yourself. Do the best that you can and help others. And get in and activate. If you don't like it, change it."

Many women spoke of the importance of having, and being, a loving partner. Susan, age fifty-six, has been in a relationship for the past three years. She described the importance of honoring partnerships.

> My advice would be to find a woman you love and say to the world, this is the woman I love and we're partners and we're together, and to keep on saying that, to honor her and to honor your relationship and the essence of your self-worth.

Ann, age seventy-one, believes that self-knowledge and acceptance are critical to being able to successfully relate to others, including a partner. She suggested an important element in creating a strong, loving partnership: self-respect.

> I think that learning self-respect—I think there are some people who maybe pursue a lot of relationships because they don't have self-respect. And having self-respect goes with something that is yours, an internal—it doesn't have anything to do with what society has to say; it's within you, and I think that that's very important. And I think that knowing that you can be truly loved by another woman—I mean, it isn't what society says out there; Pat Buchanan's family values and all that garbage that they try to dish on everyone—and you feel like, heavens, if I don't swallow all this, I'm a fifth-rate person or whatever they want you to feel like. I think that it's really knowing that you can love a woman and a woman can love you, and that can be the most wonderful love, and that's using "love" not just in [terms of] sex, but in respecting each other and having that wonderful intimacy that comes with touching. We reach over and touch each other—just when I'm driving the car, we're going along, I'll reach over and pat her on the head. And I think that's a warmth that you can find if you have truly found a really good partner and then what the two of you can build together is worth finding that person.

Coming of age and the prospect of coming out in a homophobic society strongly influenced how the women in this study approached their lives. The fear of discovery, rejection, or worse, was a constant reality. In her advice to younger lesbians, Elaine, age fifty-seven, emphasized the need for courage.

> The thing that comes to mind is, don't be afraid. I don't know quite what that means, but I think we all go through our own issues in coming out and going through the era that we grew up in, and I can remember being terrified, and you can't tell someone not to feel what they're going to feel. But I'd almost say, just hang in there; you'll get through it, and you come out on the other end and you're going to be clear. You're going to be happy. And it's not going to be easy, but when you reach the other end of the tunnel, so to speak, and you walk out into the beautiful meadow, it's going to be worth it. So just hang in there, and whatever that means to you in your personal life or professional life or whatever you're dealing with, just do it. Hang in there.

Chapter 8

Conclusion

The universal wisdom I would give to anyone—any lesbian or anyone else—I would tell them to love themselves and to thine own self be true.

Laura, age fifty-seven

An intergenerational reality permeates the lives of the lesbian elders in this study and marks their place in the world. With their years came a sense of being truly settled in the present, yet they acutely understood the need for change in the future. Deeply satisfied with their lives and with being gay, the women were vibrant, diverse, and active. Through their resilience, they brought an adaptive flexibility and resourcefulness to creating successful and gratifying lives for themselves and for those they love.

The importance of the generational and historical context of these women's lives cannot be overstated. Understanding the periods during which the women came of age and first recognized their lesbianism is essential because their history continues to shape their lives today. Despite the strength and capabilities of the women we interviewed, they remain a largely invisible population in large part due to the historical conditions under which they came of age.

As highlighted throughout the book, the women came of age at a time when homosexuality was severely stigmatized and lesbian invisibility reigned. There were few public portrayals of lesbian life, and those that existed depicted a life of despair, shame, and loneliness. Mainstream society's attitudes largely governed the language the women used to describe themselves and their beliefs about how they were supposed to live their lives.

The women's orientation to life, to being gay, to being part of a community, and to aging differed depending on their age. The lives of those in their seventies to nineties who had lived a gay life at a relatively young age tended to be cloaked in silence. Most accepted the public code of silence without question. Some went even further; they adapted to the repression of the era by "blending": never mentioning or discussing their sexuality, even with one another. As one woman reminisced, "I haven't talked about it. . . . When I found partners, we never talked about it—ever. Blended in, never discussing anything."

Although these women generally had few avenues available for meeting other lesbians, they talked of their "liaisons" or the "friends" they had met ever so discreetly and, in some cases, with whom they then went on to grow old together. Most of them recognized an increased level of social acceptance, but the majority made it clear that the closet door that had never opened would remain shut. Yet, a few of these lesbian elders, despite tremendous risk and all the societal pressures of the times—rebels, really—refused to hide or deny their lesbianism even in the very early years.

Many of the younger women—those in their mid-fifties and sixties—who had come out to themselves early in life talked of living a "double life." They came of age during a period of severe repression, when gays were publicly humiliated and persecuted. It was also a time when more avenues existed for women to meet one another including at clubs, bars, and on sports teams. With the opportunity to meet others, however, came the risk of discovery. Many lived separate gay and straight lives. They maintained a public image of heterosexuality at work and in straight society, and lived an underground lesbian life after work and on the weekends. It was important that their private lives never be made public.

Among those who had self-identified as lesbian much later in life, many were aware of their lesbian "tendencies" at a younger age, but repressed them. Often they were scared; they desperately did not want to be gay so they sought safer avenues such as marriage and motherhood. The lives of those who tried not to be gay were often marked with adversity. Some sought to escape their pain through alcohol and drug abuse or suicide attempts. If they sought help, their needs were met most often with ignorance and disapproval. They were told their homosexuality could be cured or that it was just a "phase" to be ignored and disregarded.

The women in their mid-fifties to sixties who became aware of being gay much later in life often found more support in assuming a lesbian identity. Many of these women came out within the context of the women's and gay liberation movements in the late 1960s and 1970s. Both the gay liberation movement and the women's movement provided social support and a social context that countered the homophobia of the previous fifty years. With increased cultural acceptance came added social support. Even when seeking professional help, many of the women found new levels of acceptance and assistance to live their lives. For the majority of the women in this study, however, it was too late. Their secrecy and denial were so ingrained that despite societal changes and more accepting attitudes, they were not comfortable with the increased visibility—and perceived vulnerability—that accompanied coming out.

Despite age differences, all of the women shared the reality of being different, and each had to struggle to varying degrees to come to terms with her own identity. Although sexual orientation was a primary aspect of personal identity for most of the women, many also talked of the importance of other identities, such as their racial and ethnic heritage, professional identity, and their spirituality. With resiliency and resourcefulness, they all faced a similar paradox in their daily lives: There was a cost to being themselves and a cost not to being themselves. This irony created conditions for contradictions, compromises, adversity—and strength.

Once they accepted being gay, most talked of experiencing a deep sense of relief. Some described a feeling of coming home and finally achieving a sense of belonging. As one woman shared,

> It was like coming from the stage of the cocoon to a butterfly. It's a process. It's like from one way of being to another way of being. And, more than that, though, it was to know who I was— really know who I was for the first time. Just—ah! It was like an "aha."

The women traveled unique paths to self-acceptance. The particular journey each woman walked was influenced by a number of factors, such as her individual temperament and personality, the historical context when she first recognized her lesbianism, her life circumstances, the support she received, and the critical turning points she experienced in life.

The overwhelming influence of the family and the broader culture was evident in the women's stories. Early life experiences exerted a powerful influence throughout the lives of these women. Some parents offered encouragement, a loving environment, and promoted a "can-do" attitude. Other women were met with parental disapproval, disregard, or abuse. As the women entered into lesbian relationships, a few parents provided support; most refused to acknowledge the obvious; some completely disowned their daughters.

For the women in this study, the concept of family had evolved over time. For many of the women growing up in the 1930s and 1940s, norms were set for a future of marriage, children, and grandchildren. Consequently, as young women, most defined families simply through biology or marriage, and the majority maintained connections with family members even when this required silence and disrespect. Over time, though, many parents and other family members became more accepting of the women's sexual orientation and their relationships. In the later years, most had buried their parents or were caring for their parents as they aged. Regardless of the relationship they had with their parents, the women generally came to a place of acceptance of their parents' strengths and shortcomings. They talked about the entirety of their relationships with their parents changing over the course of time.

Now, in their later years, most identified family as those who offered support, acceptance, and love through good times and bad times. Family was important to these women. The majority of them developed a dynamic yet enduring network, including partners, children, friends, relatives—a chosen family—that provided acceptance and validation. The women rarely relied on a single source of support, but rather garnered support from multiple sources. Partners were a primary source of support, with some long-term relationships spanning more than sixty years. Many had children, and motherhood and grandparenthood continued to be significant in their lives. All of the women with children showed a desire for understanding and acceptance from their children, and most felt they had strong and positive relationships with their children, as well as grandchildren.

Other important sources of support included networks of friends, church groups, volunteer groups, twelve-step programs, lesbian support groups, and various other political and community groups. The women recognized the importance of support in their lives as a key to their self-fulfillment. Without it, they may not have had the strength to be true to themselves. From such support grew internal strength— fostering self-confidence and the drive needed to overturn the barriers society placed in their way.

This was a highly self-sufficient group of women, who tended to achieve personal and professional success despite the numerous obstacles they faced. The security of their livelihood was of paramount importance, and work played a prominent role in their lives. Many lived through the Depression and, for a few, poverty was an overriding aspect of growing up. The women who had recognized their lesbianism early in life knew that they needed to provide for themselves. They were well aware of the reality of discrimination, and they worked hard to succeed in their working lives, not wanting to jeopardize their success through the discovery of being gay. Some used a "cover," such as dating men, to ensure their professional successes.

Despite rampant homophobia, workplaces—including the military—provided an opportunity for women to meet one another. However, the danger of being discovered was ever present and the consequences were severe. Most of these older lesbians accepted the need for secrecy and double lives as they learned to live with the constant fear of exposure. Despite the obstacles and stresses they faced, almost all of the women reported satisfaction from their work. Some looked forward to working as long as possible, while others looked forward to retirement. A few of the women were very concerned about ever being financially able to retire.

For a great number of those interviewed, however, their working years were well behind them and in retirement they were free to be more open about being lesbian as well as to find satisfaction in other endeavors such as volunteer work, travel, and relationships. Retirement provided an opportunity for the women to be themselves more openly and to have the time to pursue their own interests. As one woman commented,

> This is the best period in my life. I feel like I can be myself and I don't care whether people accept me or not. I'm accepted by the people who are important to me and that's all I really care about.

In their later years these women tended to face the joys and challenges of aging with a certain flexibility and adaptiveness. Having already dealt with a major shift in their identities, most brought resourcefulness to their older years. Long and challenging lives shone through in the women's perspectives on aging and the future. Having confronted adversity helped position these women for their later years. They faced the reality of their aging with a certain frankness and optimism. Whether they currently were experiencing challenges or knew they would in the future, most had an ingrained sense of fortitude, knowing that they would carry on despite the obstacles they might face. As they aged and retired, many of the women found a new sense of freedom.

The women were settled in their lives, and they honored their life choices. Their orientation toward aging and old age depended in large part on their current age as well as the specific issues they faced in their individual lives. The older women faced daily the needs and joys associated with aging and believed these were indicative of what to expect in the future. For many of the younger women, aging was simply something to be anticipated, although those with serious health problems were already facing serious challenges. To provide the security and support needed for independence as they aged, maintaining mutual support was a priority among these women. Because they acknowledged a need for a strong support system as they aged, most were hopeful that their support networks would continue to be available to them.

They faced the reality of their own aging with both concern and hope. Their primary concerns centered on their financial security, physical health, mental acuity, housing, caregiving, and decision-making. Overall, they expressed an ardent desire to remain independent. Many of their concerns were similar to people in general as they age, but as older lesbians they also had some unique needs. As lesbians, they were particularly concerned about their lack of access to supportive housing, the need to ensure control over their own lives and choices, and the importance of providing legal protection for their partners and other family members. These unique needs illustrate the importance of developing appropriate and sensitive aging services in the lesbian community as well as the community at large.

The women featured in this book indicate that services will need to be developed with a clear understanding and respect for their lives and choices. The lesbian elders we spoke with were heterogeneous in terms of age, culture, ability, income, and self-definitions. Therefore, services will need to be developed that are responsive to this diversity. The majority of these women will most likely remain independent as long as possible and refrain from receiving outside assistance in part due to a lived history of oppression and discrimination. Among those needing services, many of the older lesbians in this book will most likely receive services within traditional aging agencies and not openly identify as lesbian.

Sensitivity and training is necessary to carefully listen to the women to truly understand their life circumstances. As we provide opportunities for these women to receive assistance, it will be possible only if our language and the services we offer are respectful and inclusive of their life experiences. We need to ask who is important to them and with whom they have shared their lives as opposed to if they are or have been married. The women may also need special assistance to ensure legal protection for themselves, their partners, and other extended family members. Such legal planning is absolutely necessary to ensure that their life choices are honored and that those they love have access during times of serious illness or disability and that their life partners are fully recognized at the time of their deaths.

The younger women we interviewed will likely be more comfortable using aging-related services in the lesbian community and will be more assertive about their needs and rights as older lesbians. Service providers in the lesbian and gay community will also need to receive training regarding aging issues to ensure sensitivity and appropriate assistance. In either case, access to affordable services is critical. Many of the women that we talked with simply could not afford to pay for services.

Advocacy is also necessary to change public policies to fully recognize older lesbians and their families, to provide social security disability and survivor benefits, to protect against all types of discrimination such as in employment and housing, and to ensure full access to other public benefits. Older lesbians may be one of the most vulnerable groups of the growing aging population. The aging and lesbian and gay communities need to recognize their needs and take active steps to ensure inclusion and support. It will be important to engage the older women themselves to ensure they have an active role in service development and delivery. Lesbian elders have tremendous talents to be shared and experiences to be honored.

Many of the women we interviewed faced tremendous hardships as they sought to overcome the difficulties that accompanied being lesbian in the repressive homophobic and patriarchal society of their day. Even when they experienced extreme difficulties—being disowned by parents, losing a job, enduring a military interrogation or discharge, facing the damage created by alcoholism, or surviving the death of a partner—rarely did such hardships define their lives. Rather, they became threads woven among many other life experiences. Their stories reflect their survival and even their triumph in the face of great obstacles. How did they do it?

They took control of their lives. Cultivating rich sources of support, strengthening their own internal resources, and finding a larger meaning in life helped these women triumph over the difficult times in their lives. One of the greatest sources of strength and support for the women came from within. They tended to cultivate a strong sense of self and inner strength as they faced and overcame the adversity in their lives. Others credit their relationships or their spirituality with providing essential strength and support. A few had lesbian mentors to ease the way, but most learned through individual trial and error. Their courage and tenacity in the struggle to discover and be who they are cannot help but inspire our respect and admiration. They did what needed to be done to be independent and to accomplish their goals. They are all survivors and, generally, they are proud of who they are.

Many of the women had faced turning points in their lives that helped them to better know themselves and their place in the world. For some, these key events occurred when they were young; most happened later in life. Important turning points included facing serious illness, recognizing mortality or impending death, or surviving the death of a loved one. Many of the subsequent life changes related to how the women found meaning in their lives. Some reported that facing serious illness or death compelled them to clarify what is most important in life. Despite the pressures and the imagined as well as actual negative consequences of living as lesbians, these women persevered—loving women, seeking and finding answers to who they are, and following the rhythm of their own hearts.

Many found meaning and purpose in their lives through their relationship with God or other spiritual practices. For others, meaning was created through a commitment to their personal relationships or through community involvement—helping to build a better world. Meaning was also found in the little things in everyday life. As one woman stated,

> Every day there's something beautiful. . . . I think that's the thing that's held me together all my life, whether it's that you see a flower or running the dog or you get to hear kids laughing or even watch the squirrels scramble in the trees out there. There's something always that holds me and holds me up. That gives me meaning. Having the capacity to be me.

As we move forward in our quest to consider fully the lives of older lesbians, it is time to seek more depth and move beyond descriptive, cursive accounts and to begin providing opportunities for deepening our understanding of specific aspects of their lives, such as retirement, sexuality, grandparenthood, or "widowhood," to name a few. As we look for commonalities and shared experienced, we must not lose sight of the heterogeneity within this community. It is as diverse as it is rich in varied life experiences.

It will be important to find ways to reach out further to this largely hidden population and to make additional efforts to ensure that the diversity of the community is included in our efforts. We need to hear more from older lesbians of color, those of various religious and spiritual beliefs, and those of all abilities and disabilities. We need to develop new ways to access those who remain hidden. Those who are the hardest to reach are those we hear from the least. Their stories continue to go untold and will soon be lost to history. We need to invite them into a participatory process to ensure their stories are told and to allow our ideas and ourselves to be transformed.

Although these women developed much strength through the adversity they faced, they also knew intimately the costs of forbidden love, and many were adamant that they would never reveal their lesbianism. Yet these same women were still willing to participate in this project. Why? As elders, these women want the world to be a better place for those who follow them—for their own children and for younger gays and lesbians. These women want to contribute in building that world. Although most felt that the gay liberation movement had minimal effects in their lives, they were grateful for the positive effects in the lives of younger gays and lesbians. Multigenerational connections are needed in a community that has long been denied its history. Passing on knowledge and values is an important tool to creating a healthy community and world.

Most of the women spoke of an acceptance of both the joys and the struggles they experienced as they lived and aged. The diversity in their lives, their concerns, and their dreams reflected the range of their lived experiences. Overall, these women defied common stereotypes. Contrary to popular myth, the vast majority were satisfied, engaged in life, and enjoyed loving and supportive relationships. Their lives reflected resourcefulness, capacities and strengths forged often through hardship and adversity. Although most of the women fared well despite the difficulties they encountered, not all triumphed over the obstacles they faced. Some of the women clearly lived with deep scars created by prejudice, hatred, and oppression. Unfortunately, there are undoubtedly unheard voices—those who could not fight back, who internalized the shame and despair, who lived a life of deprivation, or who did succeed in killing themselves. The women who were the most isolated and suffered the most may be the hardest to reach. Countless other women are still trying to be something they are not, to live a lie to themselves and to the world around them.

Prior to their involvement in this project, most of the women had never had an opportunity to voice themselves publicly or simply to talk about their lives this way. In fact, many were elated that someone was actually interested in their life stories. As one woman shared, "This is so exciting that I get to contribute to my community." All of the women had advice they wanted to share with younger lesbians, and most often their advice centered on the importance of being true to oneself. Their shared experience as lesbians brought to the surface consistent messages for women who will follow them: the importance of love, self-truth, and pride figured prominently in their advice to those who will follow. One woman recommended, "Don't be afraid. You're entitled to be who you are." Another woman shared this advice: "Honesty. That's my first thing. Being able to be yourself. Not be frightened about it, and being able to defend yourself. If you've got to fight, do it. Just do it." Still another woman offered this guidance: "The universal wisdom I would give to anyone—any lesbian or anyone else—I would tell them to love themselves and to thine own self be true."

Despite the repression of the times, the women did manage to find "others of their kind" and to live lesbian lives. As the public perception of homosexuality changed, the role played by these women in bringing about change has unfortunately often been overlooked. The very act of finding each other—loving each other, meeting together when it was illegal to do so—was, intentionally or not, a powerful political step. Without them, Stonewall and gay liberation would not, and could not, have occurred.

Only through listening to the voices of these women can we learn about their experiences and our collective history, and come to appreciate their strengths and needs as they age. These women are the forerunners to the gay liberation movement; without their sacrifices and resolve, we could not be where we are today. Through looking back and looking forward, the women shared their lives—the dreams, the compromises, and the simple truths that wove together to form a long life, well lived. These are strong women who created fulfilling lives for themselves and those they love. With strength and dignity they are well poised for the future. As one woman shared, "My strength comes from the desire. . . . I have a desire to grow in grace."

Appendix A

Historical Time Line

Oscar Wilde's *The Importance of Being Earnest* is performed for the first time. It contains two bachelors who lead double lives: one in town, and one in the country. Four months later Wilde is arrested for committing "acts of gross indecency with another male person." After sensation-causing trials, he is convicted and sentenced to two years hard labor.	1894	
	1897	Havelock Ellis publishes *Sexual Inversion,* which is banned in Britain as obscene. Ellis's work is part of the medicalization of homosexuality. Sexual inversion was another name for homosexuality.
Lesbians no longer invisible. Boston marriages and women's friendships looked at for possible perversion and/or corruption.	1910	
	1914-1918	World War I

Prepared by Pat Freeman, PhD, and David Schulz, PhD, for The Northwest Lesbian and Gay History Museum Project, Seattle, Washington, and used with their permission.

1915

Radical activist Emma Goldman on a cross-country speaking tour, defends lesbianism and homosexuality. Goldman's appearances prompted many women, unhappy with having to hide their lesbianism, to share their stories with her. *(Out of the Past)*

1917

U.S. troops sent to Europe. The arrival of the "dough-boys" tips the war in favor of the Allied powers. World War I marks emergence of the United States as a world power and helps further the transformation of U.S. society from agrarian to urban.

U.S. immigration law is modified to ban "persons with abnormal sexual instincts" from entering the United States. (see *Out of the Past*)

For the first time many previously isolated gay men and women meet each other at home and abroad. At war's end (1918) some stay in European cities such as Paris and Berlin. Others stay in cities where they demobilized such as New York and Chicago.

1919

The Great Red Scare occurs.

The Newport Naval Station, Rhode Island, scandal erupts over the use of entrapment by the navy of effeminate gay sailors who are then charged with criminal acts of sodomy. The masculine men they serviced were not so charged.

1924

First known gay rights organization founded in Chicago by Henry Gerber. In 1925 his home is raided and his papers are confiscated. He and other members are arrested and held in jail for three days without charge. As a result of the arrest he loses his job and the society disbands. Gerber continues his activism through letters signed Parisex. (see *Out of the Past*)

1925 Ma Rainey is arrested at her home in Harlem for having a lesbian party. Bessie Smith bails her out the next day. Rainey and Smith are part of a large circle of African-American lesbian/bisexual women in Harlem. (see *Out of the Past*)

Publication of *The Well of Loneliness* in England. The book depicts the homosexuality of its central character Stephen, a woman of the British gentry. The novel focuses on Stephen's relationship with another woman as well as the growing lesbian community that existed in Paris following World War I. Banned in England, the novel is published in the United States after sensational court trials where it is judged not to be obscene. (see *Out of the Past*)   **1928**

1929 The stock market crashes and the Great Depression begins. It is marked by such disasters as bank closures and economic and industrial collapse. The Dust Bowl, hobo camps, Hoovervilles, flagpole sitters, and dance marathons become symbols of the 1930s. Conservatism grows and moral reformers target gays and lesbians, who now become extremely cautious as bars, clubs, and baths are raided—especially in the large metropolitan areas.

The Jewel Box Revue, a troupe of female impersonators, begins touring the United States from its base at the Jewel Box in Miami. The show is integrated, featuring African-American, Latino, Native American, and white performers, and is introduced by Storme DeLarverie in drag as a man. (*Out of the Past*) World War II begins in Europe.

1939

1941   In December Japan bombs Pearl Harbor. The Great Depression ends.

1941-1945   Hundreds of thousands of young men and women join the military or go to work in war plants. Now formerly isolated gays and lesbians find networks of gay and lesbians for the first time. Many women discover social and economic independence from their families.

Gays banned from the military but the policy is overlooked to maintain troop strength and continued use of gay and lesbian members' abilities.

FDR signs executive order that authorizes the internment of Japanese Americans in concentration camps.

1942

1945

At war's end, gays and lesbians are subjected to witch-hunts to clear the military of "perverts." Dishonorable discharges and the naming of names create fear and guilt. Many of those discharged remain in the major demobilization cities, such as New York, San Francisco, Los Angeles, and Seattle, adding their numbers to the already sizable gay communities.

Russia has the bomb. The Cold War begins.

1947

1948

Sexual Behavior in the Human Male is published by Kinsey. He states that 8 percent of males in the study were primarily or exclusively homosexual. In *Sexual Behavior in the Human Female* (1953) 28 percent of women in the study had erotic responses to women. The American public is shocked.

During the height of the Cold War hysteria in the 1950s, federal agencies seek to expose communists, fellow travelers, and pinko perverts.

1950

The Korean War starts. Federal and state agencies (i.e., HUAC) increase their search for commies, pinkos, perverts, and fellow travelers. Aliens and foreigners are deported en masse; gays and lesbians are fired from their jobs. The movie industry gives up its own, as Ronald Reagan names names. Universities turned on their "liberal"—just another name for communist—professors. Society is wracked with fear and falls over itself in appeasing politicians and the powerful. The madness ends in 1954 with the collapse of the Army-McCarthy hearings. The hearings are televised with tremendous effect on the public. The war ends in 1953.

Confidential Magazine starts publication. It regularly exposes the homosexuality of movie stars and other prominent people.

Republicans gain control of Congress; a new conservatism is underway. The media, especially TV, promotes American values. White suburban middle-class life is shown as the "norm," with women as brainless housewives, happy to be helpmates for their husbands.

1951

Mattachine Society, a homophile organization, is founded by Harry Hay, a gay rights advocate in Los Angeles. The group published a magazine, *ONE,* the first openly gay/lesbian national publication. The group is actually quite conservative. It advocates acceptance and assimilation in mainstream society.

1953 — Evelyn Hooker publishes study that shows homosexuals are not mentally disturbed.

Del Martin and Phyllis Lyon found Daughters of Bilitis in San Francisco. It is a lesbian homophile organization. — 1955

Rosa Parks is arrested for violating Alabama segregation laws. This marks the start of the civil rights movement.

Allen Ginsberg gives a public reading of "Howl," an explicit poem about gay male sex.

1957 — The Wolfenden report is issued. It states that homosexual behavior between consenting adults in private should no longer be a criminal offense.

First national lesbian convention held in San Francisco by Daughters of Bilitis. — 1960

Homophile groups gain membership among professional middle-class homosexuals.

Having learned from other civil rights movements, younger and bolder members sponsor public demonstrations.

1961 — The Hollywood production code is revised to allow the portrayal of homosexuality in films.

Illinois becomes the first state to decriminalize homosexual contact between consenting adults. (see *Out of the Past*)

	1964 U.S. involvement in Vietnam is escalating. The United States defends its involvement by arguing the "Domino Theory" by which it was assumed that if one nation became communist others would follow.
American media broadcasts battles and incursion to an increasingly polarized American public. Widespread protests among students erupt in violence. In 1970 four students, protesting the war, are killed by the National Guard at Kent State University in Ohio. The war ends in 1975.	
	1965 Mattachine Society pickets United Nations in New York to protest Cuba's internment of gays in concentration camps. They also march outside the White House in protest of government policies that exclude homosexuals from federal employment.
Troy Perry founds the Metropolitan Community Church, a gay/lesbian church in Los Angeles.	**1968**
	1969 Patrons of the Stonewall Inn, a gay bar Greenwich Village, New York, violently resist a routine police raid. Three nights of rioting follow. These Stonewall Riots mark the beginning of a gay liberation movement. It differs significantly from the more cautious mainstream gay rights movements of the homophile organizations.

Spurred by the "sexual revolution" of the 1970s, bathhouses, porno theaters, and backroom bars flourish as places for gay men to engage in anonymous sex. Many such places especially can be found in New York and San Francisco, which by the 1980s have the largest gay communities in the country.

1970

The National Organization for Women (NOW) passes a resolution recognizing the "double oppression of lesbians [is] a legitimate concern of feminism."

In New York, The Gay Liberation Front sponsors gay and lesbian dances that draw large numbers of gays, lesbians, and their supporters. Similar events occur across the country, especially in universities.

Disco takes over the bar and music scene and changed the face of many gay bars. Once dark and furtive places, gay bars were transformed into spacious bright discos with high-tech light shows, mirror balls, and an air of celebration.

1973

The American Psychiatric Association removes homosexuality from the list of mental disorders.

Rita Mae Brown's *Rubyfruit Jungle* is published.

1974

	1975	Along with other attacks on sexist culture, lesbian feminists challenge women who identify as either "butch" or "femme." In place of these "heterosexist" stereotypes, lesbian feminists try to rethink female identity and promote women-centered relationships. Some begin separatist communities entirely exclusive of men.
Anita Bryant leads a successful campaign to repeal a gay civil rights ordinance in Dade County, Florida. The campaign receives national attention.	1977	
	1978	Harvey Milk, San Francisco's first openly gay city supervisor, is assassinated along with Mayor George Moscone by disgruntled former City Supervisor Dan White. White receives a light sentence sparking outrage among San Francisco's gays and lesbians who riot at city hall.
An estimated 125,000 people attend the first National March on Washington for gay rights.	1979	

1980

Bolstered by the election of conservative Republican Ronald Reagan as president of the United States, politically active religious right organizations assert their newly found authority. Their efforts are aimed at repealing laws allowing abortions and curbing the growing acceptance of gays and lesbians. They justify their efforts as protection of the American family and "family values." As a result of their lobbying, funding to fight AIDS through research and social service is forestalled. Adoption by openly gay parents is scrutinized. Some civil rights laws protecting gays and lesbians from discrimination are repealed.

1981

A thirty-one-year-old gay male in Los Angeles is diagnosed with *Pneumocystis carinii* pneumonia. In New York a gay man is diagnosed with Kaposi's sarcoma. Rumors of a gay cancer spread across the country. This new syndrome becomes known as Acquired Immunodeficiency Syndrome (AIDS).

1984

In response to growing proof that HIV, the virus that cause AIDS, is spread by sexual contact, San Francisco closes its bathhouses.

1986

In the landmark *Bowers v. Hardwick* case, the U.S. Supreme Court rules five to four that homosexual relations between consenting adults in the privacy of their homes are not protected under the Constitution.

	1987	The AIDS Coalition to Unleash Power (ACT UP) is founded in New York by Larry Kramer. Its radical-style activism, which employs "direct action" protests, sparks a new era of political activism in the gay and lesbian community.
The 1990s saw ever increasing gay, lesbian, bisexual, and transgender visibility. But with visibility came increasingly violent antigay, homophobic hate crimes by conservative, fundamentalist, and radical right-wingers such as the Reverend Fred "God hates Fags" Phelps.	1990s	
	1992	In Oregon, antigay Measure 9 is narrowly defeated. In Colorado, voters pass Amendment 2, which banned protection of gay civil rights. It is eventually deemed unconstitutional by the United States Supreme Court.
After attempting to remove the ban on homosexuals in the military with a presidential order, President Clinton announces a compromise policy known as "Don't Ask, Don't Tell." The policy allows gays and lesbians to serve in the military as long as they do not declare their homosexuality or engage in "homosexual conduct."	1993	
		The Hawaii Supreme Court rules that the denial of marriage licenses to same sex couples is an instance of sex discrimination and, hence, a violation of the state constitution's equal protection guarantee. The case is sent back to the trial court.

Humboldt, Nebraska: Brandon Teena, a female-to-male transgender, was beaten, raped, and murdered. The sheriff does little to investigate his murder. He blames the victim.

1996

Congress passes the "Defense of Marriage Act," which defines marriage as a union between a man and a woman, grants states the right not to recognize same-sex marriages performed in another state, and denies federal benefits to same-sex marriages.

Laramie, Wyoming: Matthew Shepard is brutally beaten, tied to a fence, and left to die; ostensibly it was a robbery. In reality it was because Matthew was gay.

1998

Sylacauga, Alabama: Two men beat and kill Billy Jack Gaither in Florida because he is gay.

2001

The Salvation Army announces it will offer benefits to same-sex partners of its employees. The announcement comes some three years after the Salvation Army turned down a $3.5 million contract with the city of San Francisco that by law would have required it to provide same-sex partner benefits.

2002

Accusations of pedophilia wrack the Catholic Church. Gay priests fear a witch-hunt.

Clinton Risetter is set on fire and dies. His killer said he did it because Risetter was gay.

Alabama Supreme Court Justice Roy Moore says that homosexuality is "an inherent evil." Antigay bias is extremely strong and very apparent in cases in southern states.

GLBTs—as a group—are part of the mainstream. Television, movies, sports, Broadway, and even politics (note the Log Cabin Republicans) all feature gays, lesbians, bisexuals, and even a transgender or two on occasion. They are everywhere.

With the new visibility comes a mobilized conservative swing, which is responsible for the rescinding of equal rights for gays legislation in a number of cities across the nation. The justice department under Attorney General John Ashcroft is pursuing the restriction of civil rights on all fronts.

Perhaps, even more threatening to the GLBT "community" is the gay and lesbian conservative movement, which advocates assimilation—conformity to a heterosexual norm—at least in appearances. There is no room for dykes, queers, transgenders, fags, sissies, leathermen, and the like.

The danger to be feared now comes also from within: It has the potential to destroy the GLBT culture and community.

Appendix B

Demographic Information

Date of Birth

1902 (1)	1926 (3)	1934 (2)	1941 (1)
1914 (1)	1927 (3)	1935 (2)	1942 (2)
1918 (1)	1928 (7)	1936 (3)	
1921 (2)	1929 (1)	1937 (3)	
1922 (1)	1931 (3)	1938 (7)	
1924 (2)	1932 (2)	1939 (4)	
1925 (2)	1933 (3)	1940 (6)	

Status

Single (22)
Partnered (40)

Ethnicity

Latina (1)
African American (1)
Native American (1)
White (59)

Education

Junior High School (1)
High School Diploma (3)

Some College (18)
BA/BS Degree (13)
Graduate Degree (27)

Place of Residence

State	Population			
	<30,000	30,000-100,000	300,000-500,000	500,000-1,000,000
Washington (22)	4	4		14
Oregon (17)	10	1	2	4
California (23)	9	4	10	

Employment Status

Working (21)
Job Hunting (2)
Retired (33)
Retired and Working (6)

Major Disability

Yes (17)
No (45)

Health

Excellent (29)
Good (29)
Fair (2)
Poor (2)

Income

	Number of persons supported		
Income level	1	2	3
<10,000	3		
10,000-19,000	7	3	
20,000-29,000	12		
30,000-39,000	6	3	
40,000-49,000	4	4	
50,000-59,000	4		
>60,000	15	1	

Appendix C

Suggested Readings

Lives of Lesbian Elders shines a light on the life experiences of older lesbians as well as on the current needs of this largely invisible population. Historical background is included to allow the reader to understand the events and experiences of which the women speak. The following suggested reading list is divided into two sections: lesbian history and lesbians and aging.

Lesbian History

Ackland,V. (1988). *For Sylvia: An Honest Account.* London: Hogarth Press.

Alsop. S. M. (1978). *Lady Sackville.* New York: Doubleday and Co.

Atkins, G. (2003). *Gay Seattle: Stories of Exile and Belonging.* Seattle: University of Washington Press.

Baker, M. (1985). *Our Three Lives: The Life of Radclyffe Hall.* New York: William Morrow and Co.

Barrett, M. B. (1989). *Invisible Lives.* New York: William Morrow and Co.

Bennett, B. T. (1991). *Mary Diana Dods: A Gentleman and a Scholar.* New York: William Morrow and Co.

Benstock, S. (1986). *Women of the Left Bank: Paris 1900-1940.* Austin: University of Austin Press.

Berube, A. (1990). *Coming Out Under Fire: The History of Gay Men and Women in World War II.* New York: The Free Press.

Bryher (1972). *The Days of Mars: A Memoir 1940-1946.* New York: Harcourt Brace Jovanovich.

Burns, E. (Ed.) (1973). *Staying on Alone: The Letters of Alice B. Toklas.* New York: Vintage Books.

Castell, A. (Ed.) (1947). *John Stuart Mill on Liberty.* New York: Appleton-Century-Crofts.

Chisholm, A. (1981). *Nancy Cunard: A Biography.* New York: Penguin Books.

Collis, R. (1994). *Portraits to the Wall: Historic Lesbian Lives Unveiled.* London: Cassel, Villers House.

Cook, B. W. (1992). *Eleanore Roosevelt, Volume I.* New York: Viking.

Cook, B. W. (1999). *Eleanore Roosevelt, Volume II*. New York: Viking.

Curb, R. (Ed.) (1985). *Lesbian Nuns: Breaking the Silence*. Tallahasse, FL: The Naiad Press.

D'Emilio, J. (1988). *Intimate Matters: A History of Sexuality in America*. New York: Harper and Row.

Dickson, Lovat (1975). *Radclyffe Hall and the Well of Loneliness*. New York: Charles Scribner's Sons.

Donoghue. E. (1969). *Passions Between Women: British Lesbian Culture 1668-1801*. New York: HarperCollins.

Donovan, J. (1980). *Sarah Orne Jewett*. New York: Frederick Ungar Publishing Co.

Duberman, M. (1993). *Stonewall*. New York: Dutton.

Duberman, M., Viginus, M., and Chauncey, G., Jr. (1989). *Hidden from History: Reclaiming the Gay and Lesbian Past*. New York: NAL Books.

Faber, D. (1980). *The Life of Lorena Hickok, E.R.'s Friend*. New York: William Morrow and Co.

Faderman, L. (1981). *Surpassing the Love of Men*. New York: William Morrow and Co.

Faderman, L. (1983). *Scotch Verdict: Miss Pirie and Miss Woods versus Dame Cumming Gordon*. New York: Quill.

Faderman, L. (1991). *Odd Girls and Twilight Lovers: A History of Lesbian Life in 20th Century America*. New York: Columbia University Press.

Faderman, L. (1994). *Chloe Plus Olivia: An Anthology of Lesbian Literature from the 17th Century to the Present*. New York: Viking.

Faderman, L. (1994). *Lesbians in Germany: 1890's-1920's*. The Naiad Press.

Field, A. (1983). *Djuna: The Life and Times of Djuna Barnes*. New York: G.P. Putnam's Sons

Fischer, E. (1983). *Aimee and Jaguar: A Love Story, Berlin 1943*. New York: HarperCollins.

Fitch, N. R. (1983). *Sylvia Beach and the Lost Generation*. New York: W.W. Norton and Co.

Flanner, J. (1980). *Darlinghissima: Letters to a Friend*. New York: William Morrow and Co.

Gershick, Z. Z. (1998). *Gay Old Girls*. Los Angeles: Alyson Publications.

Glascow, J. (Ed.) (1997). *Your John: The Love Letters of Radclyffe Hall*. New York: New York University Press.

Glendinning, V. (1983). *Vita: A Biography of Vita Sackville-West*. New York: Alfred A. Knopf.

Gordon, M. (2000). *Voluptuous Panic: The Erotic World of Weimar Berlin*. Los Angeles: Feral House.

Grau, G. (Ed.) (1995). *Hidden Holocaust?: Gay and Lesbian Persecution in Germany 1933-45*. New York: Cassell.

Grier, B. (1976). *Lesbian Lives: Biographies of Women from the Ladder*. Oakland, CA: Diana Press.

Griffin, G. (1993). *Heavenly Love: Lesbian Images in 20th Century Women's Writing.* New York: Manchester University Press.

Guest, B. (1984). *Herself Defined: The Poet H.D. and Her World.* New York: Doubleday and Co.

Hall, R. (1930). *The Well of Loneliness.* New York: Covici Friede Publishers.

Hahn, E. (1977). *Mabel: A Biography of Mabel Dodge Luhan.* Boston: Houghton Mifflin.

Herring, P. (1995). *Djuna: The Life and Work of Djuna Barnes.* New York: Viking.

The History Project (1998). *Improper Bostonians.* Boston: Beacon Press.

Humphry, M. A. (1988). *My Country My Right to Serve: Experiences of Gay Men and Women in the Military, World War II to the Present.* New York: HarperCollins.

Jay, K. (1988). *The Amazon and the Page: Natalie Clifford Barney and Renee Vivien.* Bloomington: Indiana University Press.

Jensen, K. I. (1999). *Lesbian Epiphanies: Women Coming Out in Later Life.* Binghamton, NY: Harrington Park Press.

Katz, J. (1976). *Gay American History: Lesbians and Gay Men in the U.S.A.* New York: Avon Books.

Kehoe, M. (1986). *Historical, Literary, and Erotic Aspects of Lesbianism.* Binghamton, NY: Harrington Park Press.

Kehoe, M. (1989). *Lesbians Over Sixty Speak for Themselves.* Binghamton, NY: Harrington Park Press.

Kennedy, E. and Davis, M. (1993). *Boots of Leather, Slippers of Gold.* New York: Routledge Inc.

Lenska, M. A. and Phillips, J. (Eds.) (1989). *Violet to Vita: The Letters of Violet Trefusis to Vita Sackville-West 1910-1921.* New York: Viking.

MacDonald, B.with Rich, C. (1981). *Look Me in the Eye: Old Women, Aging, and Ageism.* Minneapolis, MN: Spinsters Ink.

Mackay, A. (Ed.) (1993). *Wolf Girls at Vassar: Lesbian and Gay Experiences 1930-1990.* New York: St. Martin's Press.

Madsen, A. (1995). *The Sewing Circle: Hollywood's Greatest Secret; Female Stars Who Loved Other Women.* New York: Birch Lane Press Book.

Marcus, E. (1992). *Making History: The Struggle for Gay and Lesbian Rights 1845-1990.* New York: HarperCollins.

Mavor, E. (1984). *Life with the Ladies of Llangollen.* New York: Viking.

Mayen, J. (1994). *Directed by Dorothy Arzner.* Indiana: Indiana University Press.

McLellan, D. (2000). *The Girls.* New York: St. Martin's Press.

McDougal, R. (1976). *The Very Rich Hours of Adrienne Monier.* New York: Charles Scribner's Sons.

Mellow, J. R. (1974). *Charmed Circle: Gertrude Stein and Company.* New York: Praeger Publishers.

Melville, J. (1987). *Ellen and Eddy.* New York: Routledge Inc.

Miller, N. (1995). *Out of the Past: Gay and Lesbian History from 1869 to the Present.* New York: Vintage Books.

Newton, E. (1993). *Cherry Grove, Fire Island: Sixty Years in America's First Gay and Lesbian Town.* Boston: Beacon Press.

Nicholson, N. (Ed.) (1992). *Vita and Harold: The Letters of Vita Sackville-West and Harold Nicholson.* New York: G.P. Putnam's Sons.

Oldfield, S. (1993). *Spinsters of the Parish: The Life and Times of F.M. Mayor and Mary Sheepshanks.* London: Virago Press, Ltd.

Ormrod, R. (1985). *Una Troubridge: The Friend of Radclyffe Hall.* New York: Carroll and Graf Publishers, Inc.

Paulson, D. (1996). *An Evening at the Garden of Allah: A Gay Cabaret in Seattle.* New York: Columbia University Press.

Pettis, R. (Ed.) (2002). *Mosaic 1: Life Stories from Isolation to Community.* Seattle, WA: Northwest Lesbian and Gay History Museum Project.

Phelps, R. (1978). *Belle Saisons: A Collete Scrapbook.* New York: Farrar Straus.

Phelps, R. (1980). *Letters from Colette.* New York: Farrar Straus Giroux.

Richards, D. (1993). *Superstars: Twelve Lesbians Who Changed the World.* New York: Carroll and Graf Publishers.

Robinson, J. (1982). *H.D.: The Life and Work of an American Poet.* Houghton Mifflin.

Robinson, P. (1983). *Willa: The Life of Willa Cather.* New York: Doubleday and Co.

Rodriguez, S. (2002). *Wild Heart: A Life.* New York: HarperCollins.

Schoppmann, C. (1993). *Days of Masquerade. Life Stories of Lesbians During the Third Reich.* New York: Columbia University Press.

Secrest, M. (1974). *Between Me and Life: A Biography of Romaine Brooks.* New York: Doubleday and Co.

Shilts, R. (1993). *Conduct Unbecoming: Gays and Lesbians in the U.S. Military.* New York: St. Martin's Press.

Shutts, D. (1982). *Lobotomy: Resort to the Knife.* New York: Van Nostrom Reinhold Co.

Simon, L. (1978).*The Biography of Alice B. Toklas.* New York: Avon Books.

Simon, L. (1994). *Gertrude Stein Remembered.* Lincoln: University of Nebraska Press.

Smith, J. S. (1982). *Elsie de Wolfe.* New York: Atheneum.

Solomon, B. M. (1985). *In the Company of Educated Women.* New Haven, CT: Yale University Press.

Souhami, D. (1988). *Gluck.* London: Pandora Press.

Souhami, D. (1991). *Gertrude and Alice.* London: Pandora Press.

Souhami, D. (1996). *Mrs. Kepple and Her Daughter.* New York: St. Martin's Press.

Souhami, D. (1999). *The Trials of Radclyffe Hall.* New York: Doubleday and Co.

Steward, S. M. (Ed.) (1977). *Dear Sammy: Letters from Gertrude Stein and Alice B. Toklas.* Boston: Houghton Mifflin.

Streitmatter, R. (Ed.) (1998). *Empty Without You: The Intimate Letters of Eleanore Roosevelt.* New York: The Free Press.

Stryker, S. (1996). *Gay by the Bay: A History of Queer Culture in the San Francisco Bay Area*. San Francisco: Chronicle Books.

Thurman, J. (1999). *Secrets of the Flesh: A Life of Colette*. New York: Alfred A. Knopf.

Toklas, A. B. (1954). *The Alice B. Toklas Cook Book*. New York: Harper and Row.

Toklas, A. B. (1985). *What Is Remembered*. San Francisco: North Point Press.

Van Gelder, L. (1996). *The Girls Next Door*. New York: Simon and Schuster.

von Krafft-Ebing, R. (1969). *Psychopathia Sexualis*. Translated by F. S. Klaf. New York: Bantam Books.

Weiss, A. (1992). *Vampires and Violets: Lesbians in Film*. New York: Penguin Books.

Wells, A. M. (1978). *Miss Marks and Miss Wooley*. Boston: Houghton Mifflin.

Whitbread, H. (1992). *No Priest but Love: Excerpts from the Diaries of Anne Lister*. New York: New York University Press.

Wickes, G. (1976). *The Amazon of Letters: The Life and Loves of Natalie Barney*. New York: G.P. Putnam's Sons.

Wilde, O. (1960). *DeProfundis*. Edited by V. Holland. New York: The Philosophical Library.

Wineapple, B. (1989). *Genet: A Biography of Janet Flanner*. New York: Ticknor and Fields.

Witt, L., Thoms, S., and Marcus, E. (1995). *Out in All Directions*. New York: Warner Books.

Lesbians and Aging

Adelman, M. (Ed.) (1986). *Lesbian Passages: True Stories Told by Women Over 40*. Los Angeles: Alyson Publications.

Adelman, M. (Ed.) (1986). *Long Time Passing: Lives of Older Lesbians*. Los Angeles: Alyson Publications.

Adelman, M. (1990). Stigma, gay lifestyles and adjustment to aging: A study of later-life gay men and lesbians. *Journal of Homosexuality* 20(3/4): 7-32.

Auger, J. A. (1992). Living in the margins: Lesbian aging. *Canadian Womens' Studies* 12(2): 80-84.

Bell, A. P. and Weinberg, M. S. (1978). *Homosexualities*. New York: Simon and Schuster.

Bell, A. P., Weinberg, M. S., and Hammersmith, S. K. (1981). *Sexual Preference: Its Development in Men and Women*. Bloomington, IN: Indiana University Press.

Berger, R. M. (1982). The unseen minority: Older gays and lesbians. *Social Work* 21: 236-242.

Berger, R. M. (1984). Realities of gay and lesbian aging. *Social Work* 29(1): 57-62.

Berger, R. M. (1985). Rewriting a bad script: Older lesbians and gays. In H. Hidalgo, T. L. Peterson, and N. J. Woodman (Eds.), *Lesbian and Gay Issues: A Resource Manual for Social Workers* (pp. 53-59). Silver Spring, MD: NASW.

Berger, R. M. and Kelly, J. (1986). Working with homosexuals of the older population. *Social Casework* 67(4): 203-210.

Berger, R. M. and Kelly, J. (1996). Gay men and lesbians grown older. In R. P. Cabaj and T. S. Stein (Eds.), *Textbook of Homosexuality and Mental Health* (pp. 305-311). Washington, DC: American Psychiatric Press.

Bland, J. A. (2001). Twice hidden: Older gay and lesbian couples, friends, and intimacy. *Generations* 25(2): 87-89.

Boxer, A. M. (1997). Gay, lesbian, and bisexual aging into the twenty-first century: An overview and introduction. *Journal of Gay, Lesbian, and Bisexual Identity* 2(34): 187-197.

Cahill, S. and South, K. (2002). Policy issues affecting lesbian, gay, bisexual, and transgender people in retirement. *Generations* 26(2): 49-54.

Carlson, H. M. and Steuer, J. (1985). Age, sex-role categorization, and psychological health in American homosexual and heterosexual men and women. *Journal of Social Psychology* 125: 203-211.

Castleman, M. (1981). Growing older homosexual. *Medical Self-Care Magazine* 15 (Winter): 20.

Connolly, L. (1996). Long-term care and hospice: The special needs of older gay men and lesbians. *Journal of Gay and Lesbian Social Services* 5(1): 77-91.

Cook-Daniels, L. (1997). Lesbian, gay male, bisexual, and transgendered elders: Elder abuse and neglect issues. *Journal of Elder Abuse and Neglect* 9(2): 35-49.

Copper, B. (1980). On being an older lesbian. *Generations* 25(2): 39-40.

Cruikshank, M. (1991). Lavender and gray: A brief survey of lesbian and gay aging studies. *Journal of Homosexuality* 20(3/4): 77-87.

D'Augelli, A. R., Grossman, A. H., Hershberger, S. L., and O'Connell, T. S. (2001). Aspects of mental health among older lesbian, gay and bisexual adults. *Aging and Mental Health* 5(2): 149-158.

Davidson, J. K., Sr. and More, N. B. (Eds.) (2001). *Speaking of Sexuality: Interdisciplinary Readings.* Los Angeles: Roxbury Publishing Co.

Dawson, K. (1982). Serving the older gay community. *SEICUS Report* November: 5-6.

Deevey, S. (1990). Older lesbian women: An invisible minority. *Journal of Gerontological Nursing* 16(5): 35-39.

Delaney, D. D. and Kelly, J. (1982). Improving services to gay and lesbian clients. *Social Work* 21(2): 178-183.

Denzin, N. K. and Lincoln, Y. S. (Eds.) (1994). *Handbook of Qualitative Research.* Thousand Oaks, CA: Sage.

Donovan, T. (2001). Being transgender and older: A first person account. *Journal of Gay and Lesbian Social Services* 13(4): 19-22.

Dorfman, R., Walters, K., Burke, P., Harding, L., Karanik, T., Raphael, J., and Silverstein, E. (1995). Old, sad, and alone: The myth of the aging homosexual. *Journal of Gerontological Social Work* 24(1-2): 29-43.

Ehrenberg, M. (1996). Aging and mental health: Issues in the gay and lesbian community. In C. J. Alexander (Ed.), *Gay and Lesbian Mental Health: A Sourcebook for Practitioners* (pp. 189-209). Binghamton, NY: The Haworth Press.

Fairchild, S. K., Carrino, G. E., and Ramirez, M. (1996). Social workers' perspectives of staff attitudes toward resident sexuality in a random sample of New York State University homes: A pilot study. *Journal of Gerontological Social Work* 26(1/2): 153-169.

Fenwick, R. D. (1978). Chapter 6: Perspectives on aging. In *The Advocate Guide to Gay Health* (pp. 136-167). New York: E. P. Dunton.

Friend, R. A. (1987). The individual and social psychology of aging: Clinical implications for lesbians and gay men. *Journal of Homosexuality* 14(1-2): 307-331.

Friend, R. A. (1989). Older lesbian and gay people: Responding to homophobia. *Marriage and Family Review* 14(3/4): 241-263.

Friend, R. A. (1990). Older lesbian and gay people: A theory of successful aging. *Journal of Homosexuality* 20(3/4): 99-118.

Gabbay, S. G. and Wahler, J. J. (2002). Lesbian aging: Review of a growing literature. *Journal of Gay and Lesbian Social Services* 14(3): 1-21.

Galanti, C. B. (1992). Homosexual preoccupation in a gero-psychiatric client: A case for psychoanalytically oriented therapy. *Perspectives in Psychiatric Care* 28(2): 21-24.

Galassi, F. S. (1991). A life review workshop for gay and lesbian elders. *Journal of Gerontological Social Work* 16(1-2): 75-86.

Gidlow, E. (1976). A view from the seventy-seventh year. *Women: A Journal of Liberation* 4: 32-35.

Gidlow, E. (1980). Memoirs. *Feminist Studies* 6(1): 107-127.

Goldfried, M. R. (2001). Integrating gay, lesbian, and bisexual issues into mainstream psychology. *American Psychologist* 56(11): 977-988.

Greene, B. (2002). Older lesbians' concerns and psychotherapy: Beyond a footnote to the footnote. In F. K. Trotman and C. M. Brody (Eds.), *Psychotherapy and Counseling with Older Women: Cross-Cultural, Family, and End-of-Life Issues* (pp. 161-174). New York: Springer.

Grossman, A. H., D'Augelli, A. R., and Hershmerger, S. L. (2000). Social support networks of lesbian, gay, and bisexual adults 60 years of age and older. *Journal of Gerontology: Psychological Sciences* 55B(3): P171-P179.

Gwenwald, M. (1984). The SAGE model for serving older lesbians and gay men. *Journal of Social Work and Human Sexuality* 2: 53-61.

Hamburger, L. (1997). The wisdom of non-heterosexually based senior housing and related services. *Journal of Gay and Lesbian Social Services* 6(1): 11-25.

Harrison, J. (1999). A lavender pink grey power: Gay and lesbian gerontology in Australia. *Australasian Journal on Ageing* 18(1): 32-37.

Hash, K. (2001). Preliminary study of caregiving and post-caregiving experiences of older gay men and lesbians. *Journal of Gay and Lesbian Social Services* 13(4): 87-94.

Herdt, G., Beeler, J., and Rawls, T. W. (1997). Life course diversity among older lesbians and gay men: A study in Chicago. *Journal of Gay, Lesbian, and Bisexual Identity* 2(3/4): 231-246.

Hostetler, A. J. and Cohen, B. J. (1997). Partnership, singlehood, and the lesbian and gay life course: A research agenda. *Journal of Gay, Lesbian, and Bisexual Identity* 2(3/4): 199-230.

Janus, S. S. and Janus, C. L. (1993). *The Janus Report on Sexual Behavior.* New York: John Wiley and Sons.

Jay, K. and Young, A. (1979). *The Gay Report.* New York: Summit Books.

Johnson, M. T. and Kelly, J. J. (1979). Deviate sex behavior in the aging: Social definitions and the lives of older gay people. In O. J. Kaplan (Ed.), *Psychopathology of Aging* (pp. 243-258). New York: Academic Press.

Jones, B. E. (2001). Is having the luck of growing old in the gay, lesbian, bisexual, transgender community good or bad luck? *Journal of Gay and Lesbian Social Services* 13(4): 13-14.

Jones, B. E. and Hill, M. J. (Eds.) (2002). Mental health issues in lesbian, gay, bisexual, and transgender communities. *Review of Psychiatry* 21(4). Washington, DC: American Psychiatric Publishing.

Jones, T. C. and Nystrom, N. M. (2002). Looking back . . . looking forward: Addressing the lives of lesbians 55 and older. *Journal of Women and Aging* 14(3/4): 59-76.

Kehoe, M. (1986). A portrait of the older lesbian. In M. Kehoe (Ed.), *Historical, Literary, and Erotic Aspects of Lesbianism* (pp. 157-161). Binghamton, NY: Harrington Park Press.

Kehoe, M. (1986). Lesbians over 65: A triply invisible minority. In M. Kehoe (Ed.), *Historical, Literary, and Erotic Aspects of Lesbianism* (pp. 139-152). Binghamton, NY: Harrington Park Press.

Kehoe, M. (1988). Lesbians over 60 speak for themselves. *Journal of Homosexuality* 16(3/4): 1-111.

Kehoe, M. (1990). Loneliness and the aging homosexual: Is pet therapy an answer? *Journal of Homosexuality* 20(3/4): 137-142.

Kelly, J. (1980). Homosexuality and aging. In J. Marmor (Ed.), *Homosexual Behavior: A Modern Reappraisal* (pp. 176-193). New York: Basic Books.

Kimmel, D. C. (1978). Adult development and aging: A gay perspective. *Journal of Social Issues* 34(3): 113-130.

Kimmel, D. C. (1992). The families of older gay men and lesbians. *Generations* 16(3): 37-38.

Kochman, A. (1997). Gay and lesbian elderly: Historical overview and implications for social work practice. *Journal of Gay and Lesbian Social Services* 6(1), 1-10.

Laird, J. (1996). Invisible ties: Lesbians and their families of origin. In J. Laird and R. J. Green (Eds.), *Lesbians and Gays in Couples and Families: A Handbook for Therapists* (pp. 89-122). San Francisco: Jossey-Bass.

Laner, M. R. (1979). Growing older female: Heterosexual and homosexual. *Journal of Homosexuality* 4(3): 267-275.

Langley, J. (2001). Developing anti-oppressive empowering social work practice with older lesbian women and gay men. *British Journal of Social Work* 31: 917-932.

Lee, J. A. (1990). Gay midlife and maturity. *Journal of Homosexuality* (entire issue) 20(3/4).

Lipman, A. (1986). Homosexual relationships. *Generations* 10(4): 51-54.

Loewenstein, S. F. (1980). Understanding lesbian women. *Social Casework: The Journal of Contemporary Social Work* 61: 29-38.

Lucco, A. J. (1987). Planned retirement housing preferences of older homosexuals. *Journal of Homosexuality* 14(3/4): 35-56.

Martin, D. and Lyon, P. (1979). The older lesbian. In B. Berzon and R. Leighton (Eds.), *Positively Gay* (pp. 134-145). Millbrae, CA: Celestial Arts.

McDougall, G. J. (1993). Therapeutic issues with gay and lesbian elders. *Clinical Gerontologist* 14: 45-57.

Metz, P. (1997). Staff development for work with lesbian and gay elders. *Journal of Gay and Lesbian Social Services* 6(1): 35-45.

Minnigerode, F. A. and Adelman, M. R. (1978). Elderly homosexual women and men: Report on a pilot study. *Family Coordinator* (October), 451-456.

Morrow, D. F. (2001). Older gays and lesbians: Surviving a generation of hate and violence. *Journal of Gay and Lesbian Social Services* 13(1/2): 151-169.

Muhlenkamp, A. F. and Sayles, J. A. (1986). Self-esteem, social support and positive health practices. *Nursing Resources* 35: 334-338.

Nichols, M. (1989). Sex therapy with lesbians, gay men, and bisexuals. In S. R. Leiblum and R. C. Rosen (Eds.), *Principles and Practice of Sex Therapy: Update for the 1990s* (Second Edition) (pp. 269-297). New York: Guilford.

Nugent-Wells, K. (1995). Older lesbian and bisexual women of color envision ideal health care setting. *Sojourner–The Women's Forum* 20(7): 1H.

Peplau, L. A. (1981). What homosexuals want. *Psychology Today* March: 28-38.

Poor, M. (1982). Older lesbians. In M. Cruikshank (Ed.), *Lesbian Studies* (pp. 165-173). Old Westburg, NY: Feminist Press.

Quam, J. K. (1993). Gay and lesbian aging. *SIECUS Report* 21(5), 10-12.

Quam, J. K. (1997). The story of Carrie and Anne: Long-term care crisis. *Journal of Gay and Lesbian Social Services* 6(1): 97-99.

Quam, J. K. and Whitford, G. S. (1992). Adaptation and age related expectations of older gay and lesbian adults. *The Gerontologist* 32(3): 367-374.

Raphael, S. M. and Robinson, M. K. (1980). The older lesbian: Love relationships and friendship patterns. *Alternative Lifestyles* 3(2): 207-229.

Raphael, S. and Robinson (Meyer), M. (1988). The old lesbian: Some observations ten years later. In M. Shernoff and W. A. Scott (Eds.), *The Sourcebook on Lesbian/Gay Health Care* (pp. 68-72). Washington, DC: National Lesbian/Gay Health Foundation.

Reid, J. D. (1995). Development in late life: Older lesbian and gay lives. In A. R. D'Augelli and C. J. Patterson (Eds.), *Lesbian, Gay, and Bisexual Identities over the Lifespan: Psychological Perspectives* (pp. 215-240). London: Oxford.

Rosenfeld, D. (1999). Identity work among lesbian and gay elderly. *Journal of Aging Studies* 13(2): 121-144.

Sang, B., Warshow, J., and Smith, A. J. (Eds.). (1991). *Lesbians at Midlife: The Creative Transition.* San Francisco: Spinsters Ink.

Sharp, C. E. (1997). Lesbianism and later life in an Australian sample: How does development of one affect anticipation of the other? *Journal of Gay, Lesbian, and Bisexual Identity* 2(3/4): 247-263.

Shenk, D. and Fullmer, E. (1996). Significant relationship among older women: Cultural and personal constructions of lesbianism. *Journal of Women and Aging* 8(3/4): 75-89.

Slusher, M. P., Mayer, C. J., and Dunkle, R. E. (1996). Gays and Lesbians Older and Wiser (GLOW): A support group for older gay people. *The Gerontologist* 36(1): 118-123.

Stearns, D. C. and Sabini, J. (1997). Dyadic adjustment and community involvement in same-sex couples. *Journal of Gay and Lesbian Social Services* 2(3/4): 265-283.

Sussman, S.C. (2001). Vision and older adults. *Journal of Gay and Lesbian Social Services: Issues in Practice, Policy and Research* 13(4): 95-101.

Thompson, K. M., Brown, N., Cassidy, J., and Gentry, J. H. (1999). Lesbians discuss beauty and aging. *Journal of Lesbian Studies* 3(4): 37-44.

Vida, G. (Ed.) (1996). *The New Our Right to Love: A Lesbian Resource Book.* New York: Simon and Schuster.

Whalen, D. M., Bigner, J. J., and Barber, C. E. (2000). The grandmother role as experienced by lesbian women. *Journal of Women and Aging* 12(3-4): 39-57.

Whitbourne, S. K., Jacobo, M., and Munoz-Ruiz, M. T. (1996). Adversity in the lives of the elderly. In R. S. Feldman (Ed.), *The Psychology of Adversity* (pp. 160-181). Amherst, MA: University of Massachusetts Press.

Wirth, S., Eversley, R., and Rubin, N. (1981). Lesbian and gay issues. *Catalyst* 3(4): 5-117.

Wojciechowski, C. (1998). Issues in caring for older lesbians. *Journal of Gerontological Nursing* 24(7): 28-38.

Yoakam, J. (1997). Playing Bingo with the best of them: Community initiated programs for older gay and lesbian adults. *Journal of Gay and Lesbian Social Services* 6(1): 27-34.

Index

Order a copy of this book with this form or online at:
http://www.haworthpress.com/store/product.asp?sku=5213

LIVES OF LESBIAN ELDERS
Looking Back, Looking Forward

_____ in hardbound at $29.95 (ISBN: 0-7890-2333-4)

_____ in softbound at $16.95 (ISBN: 0-7890-2334-2)

Or order online and use special offer code HEC25 in the shopping cart.

COST OF BOOKS_____	☐ **BILL ME LATER:** (Bill-me option is good on US/Canada/Mexico orders only; not good to jobbers, wholesalers, or subscription agencies.)
POSTAGE & HANDLING_____ *(US: $4.00 for first book & $1.50 for each additional book) (Outside US: $5.00 for first book & $2.00 for each additional book)*	☐ Check here if billing address is different from shipping address and attach purchase order and billing address information. Signature_____
SUBTOTAL_____	☐ **PAYMENT ENCLOSED: $**_____
IN CANADA: ADD 7% GST_____	☐ **PLEASE CHARGE TO MY CREDIT CARD.**
STATE TAX_____ *(NJ, NY, OH, MN, CA, IL, IN, & SD residents, add appropriate local sales tax)*	☐ Visa ☐ MasterCard ☐ AmEx ☐ Discover ☐ Diner's Club ☐ Eurocard ☐ JCB Account # _____
FINAL TOTAL_____ *(If paying in Canadian funds, convert using the current exchange rate, UNESCO coupons welcome)*	Exp. Date_____ Signature_____

Prices in US dollars and subject to change without notice.

NAME_____

INSTITUTION_____

ADDRESS_____

CITY_____

STATE/ZIP_____

COUNTRY_____ COUNTY (NY residents only)_____

TEL_____ FAX_____

E-MAIL_____

May we use your e-mail address for confirmations and other types of information? ☐ Yes ☐ No
We appreciate receiving your e-mail address and fax number. Haworth would like to e-mail or fax special discount offers to you, as a preferred customer. **We will never share, rent, or exchange your e-mail address or fax number.** We regard such actions as an invasion of your privacy.

Order From Your Local Bookstore or Directly From
The Haworth Press, Inc.
10 Alice Street, Binghamton, New York 13904-1580 • USA
TELEPHONE: 1-800-HAWORTH (1-800-429-6784) / Outside US/Canada: (607) 722-5857
FAX: 1-800-895-0582 / Outside US/Canada: (607) 771-0012
E-mailto: orders@haworthpress.com

For orders outside US and Canada, you may wish to order through your local
sales representative, distributor, or bookseller.
For information, see http://haworthpress.com/distributors

(Discounts are available for individual orders in US and Canada only, not booksellers/distributors.)
PLEASE PHOTOCOPY THIS FORM FOR YOUR PERSONAL USE.
http://www.HaworthPress.com   BOF04